STEPHEN KING

~ Odds & Ends ~

Hans-Åke Lilja

BearManor Media.com

Stephen King Odds & Ends

Typesetting and layout by PKJ Passion Global

Published in the USA by
BearManor Media
1317 Edgewater Dr #110
Orlando FL 32804
www.BearManorMedia.com

Cover by Anders Jakobson

Softcover Edition
ISBN-10:
ISBN-13: 979-8-88771-757-9

Published in the USA by Bear Manor Media

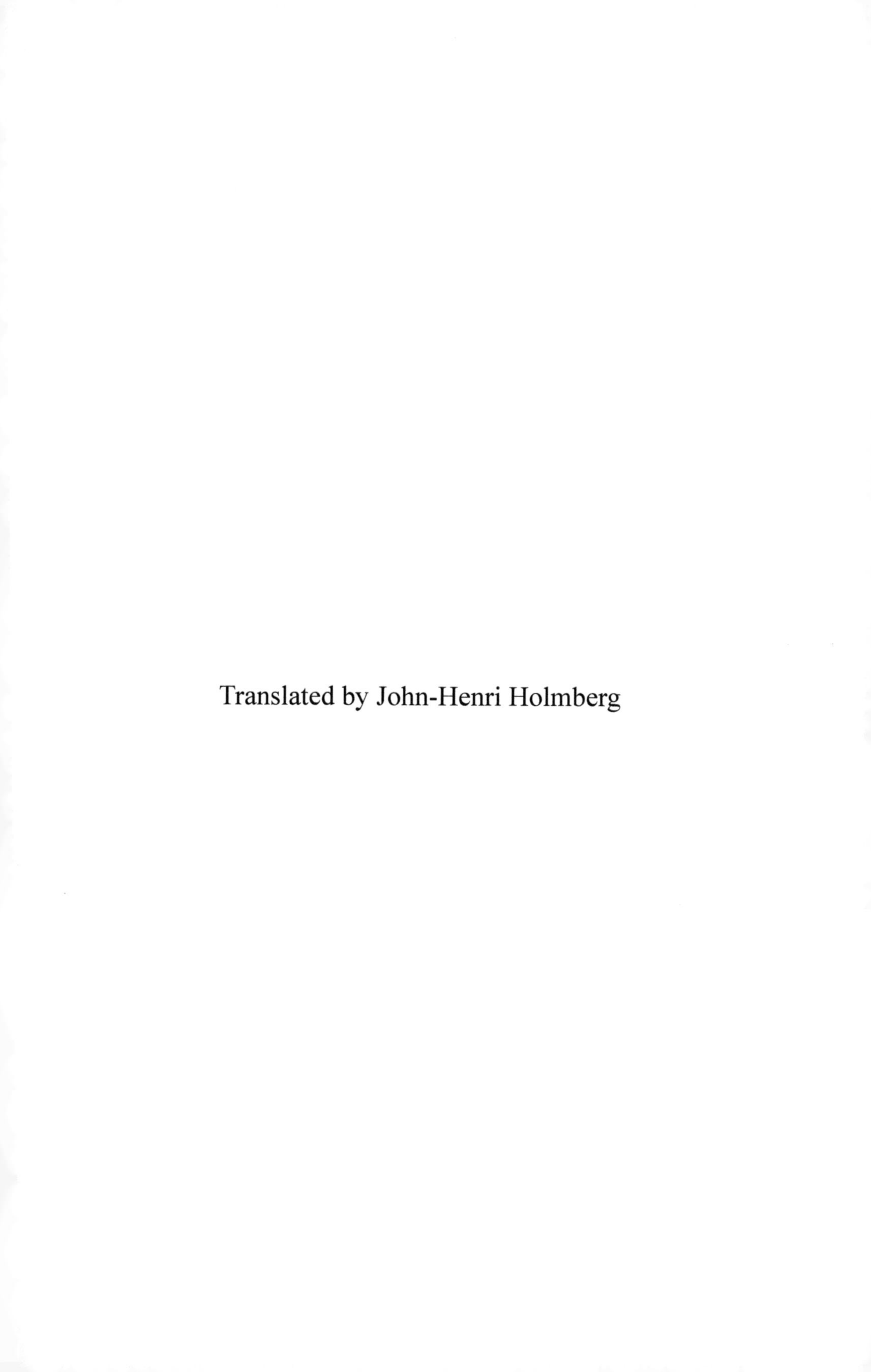

Translated by John-Henri Holmberg

Contents

To all my readers:
Many thanks! Without you,
this book would never have been written.

To Agnes and Viktor:
Damn, you really are the best!

Introduction

After finishing my book *Stephen King: Not Just Horror* (BearManor Media, 2023), I was left with many ideas I had been unable to use. Ideas which were a fine basis for further chapters, but which didn't fit into the book since they actually dealt with matters concerned with horror. So already before the book was published I knew that I had the makings of the next one. That book turned out to be *Stephen King: Stories from Five Decades of Storytelling* (BearManor Media, 2024). When it was done, I had two chapters which did not fit into the book. One of them concerned the various charities to which King contributes. The reason for that chapter being left out was that although the subject is interesting, it is also difficult to research. King is generous, but his philosophy is clearly that what matters is what they money is spent on, not who is contributing. This is certainly a noble view, but it also makes it difficult to find the necessary facts, and consequently any such discussion runs the risk of being woefully inadequate rather than reasonably adequate. This is in no way intended to convey the notion that all other chapters in my books are both totally comprehensive and void of any mistakes. I know they are not. And really, this is the difficulty when writing non-fiction as compared to running an Internet site. You can't just power up your computer and change or add things. Most publishers seem unwilling to print new editions of a book just because of a misspelled word or a book or film title having been left out of a list. So since the publishing business doesn't work that way, all that's left is doing the best you can and hope that it will be sufficient. Which all was a very roundabout way of saying that no chapter on Stephen King's generosity was included in my earlier books, nor will you find any in this one.

The second chapter left out of *King: Stories from Five Decades of Storytelling* was one on Molly, also known as The Thing of Evil: Stephen King's dog. It was included in an early draft of the book, but my friend and early reader Anders suggested that it didn't earn its place: if I remember correctly, his view was that it simply was too short to be interesting. And I agreed. So there they were, two chapters left out when the book was published. One I was unable to write and one I had written but was dissatisfied with. But at the time I felt that the two books on Stephen King I had written were enough. I really had nothing of any substance to add.

In spite of this, however, I was unable to stop jotting down the occasional idea that occurred to me. As time passed the number of ideas increased and I began feeling that perhaps there was another book to be found somewhere among them. After some further thought, I arrived at the decision to write it. I even knew what to call it: *Stephen King: From Christmas Card to Dancing Dog*. The Christmas card you'll find in the chapter on *The Plant* which opens the book, and at that time I had intended to close with a chapter on how stuntman Gary Morgan, in a Saint Bernard disguise, acted as a stand-in for Cujo in the eponymously named movie. But sad to say, there turned out to be very little to write about Mr. Morgan's adventures playing dog, so instead of ending the book with him, he has been reduced to one of the interludes in it, and since this made my imagined title impossible to use, and my book is instead called *Stephen King: (Odd) Anecdotes*, which is just an acknowledgement of the fact that it truly is a grab-bag of facts, anecdotes, and amusing tidbits. I began writing it in earnest on November 11, 2024, at the same time as I started telling my various publishers in different parts of the world of it. The work went fairly rapidly, which was lucky since the book had quickly been sold to no less than four publishers whom I had promised a manuscript sometime during the spring of 2025. Which means that I had sold them a book before having written it. Can you do that? Yes, you can, and I did.

So I wrote on, the words came and in January of 2025 it was time for my early readers to take a look. As usual, their responses were a mixture of positive and negative reactions, but some of them at least agreed on one thing (which I now realized I, too, had been uncertain about): my proposed title. I really ought to rethink it. Then, in an e-mail, John Ajvide Lindqvist suggested another title – *Stephen King: Odds and Ends*. And immediately I thought: there it is.

But how about those two surviving chapters from my previous book, someone might wonder. The one about King's philanthropy still lies fallow – or, more concretely, in my ideas folder, and is not in this book. The chapter on The Thing of Evil, however, you will find here, but just as my friend Anders suggested I have rewritten it. Hopefully he will like it better in this form. At least I do.

Hans-Åke Lilja

Christmas cards to be wished for

When I was young, it was very important to my parents, or at least my mother, that we sent Christmas cards to everyone we knew. A pile of them was bought, and unless ”Merry Christmas and a Happy New Year” was already printed on them, it was added by hand. Then everyone in the family would sign. Special Christmas stamps were bought, cheaper than ordinary ones, then everyone would have to wet and put on stamps until your tongue felt like a swollen lump in your mouth, and finally the pile was mailed off.

During the following weeks we received Christmas cards from lots of acquaintances to whom we had hopefully already sent cards. If one was received from someone we had forgotten, a new card would hurriedly be bought and mailed. If this happened too close to Christmas, the new card would just be a Happy New Year one. Great care was still taken with all of this when I was a teenager back in the 1980s.

Whether Stephen King considers it important to send Christmas cards I don't know, but I do know that he cared enough during the 1980s to write three parts of a novel, *The Plant,* in 1982, 1983, and 1985. These three little booklets were published by King's own imprint, Philtrum Press, which was run from King's office by his assistant, and were mailed out as Christmas cards. The story is set at a publishing house and is told in the form of letters, internal memos and other communications. It tells of a manuscript received by an editor which is not entirely without merit, but which includes a number of very nasty pictures of what looks like dead persons. The editor rejects the book and receives what looks like a small plant in return. A plant which then plays a major part in the rest of the story. Since King thought that the story after those first three parts began to be too similar to that of the 1960 film *The Little Shop of Horrors*, he decided not to continue it further and the "poor" recipients of his unique Christmas cards never learned what happened to the characters in the book. In 2000, King made another effort to finish *The Plant*, this time in the form of pdfs you could download from his website.

This is the deal you accepted by downloading *The Plant*. In this case, "I" stands for Stephen King, "you" for anyone downloading the story:

What I Promise

1. *To publish the first 10,000 or so words of The Plant in two installments, no matter what. Installment One goes up on this site July 24th; Installment Two will appear August 21st*
2. *If response is good and the pay-through equals or exceeds 75%, Installment Three will go up in September.*
3. *When Installment Three goes up, Installment One goes down.*
4. *If response is strong, I promise to carry The Plant through to its conclusion. I won't leave you hanging, in other words.*
5. *Above item is cancelled if I die.*
6. *If response is weak, I promise to pull the plug after Installment Two.*

++++++++++++++++++++++++++++++++++++

What You Promise

1. *To pay for each installment of The Plant, and to pay each time you download it. Look at it this way: you couldn't go into a bookstore and say, "I bought a copy of The Street Lawyer in here yesterday, so give me four more for free today." Get it?*
2. *Not to print extra copies and sell them to your friends. If you want to print copies and give them away, I can't stop you (in fact I can't stop you from doing anything, which is the beauty of this*

thing – think of it as web-moshing). But don't sell them. Two reasons: first, it's against the law, and second, it's nasty behavior. Respect my copyright. As a writer, it's all I've got.

The first part of the serial was downloaded no less than 120.000 times and more than 75 per cent of those were paid for with the required one dollar. For the second part, payments fell to 70 per cent, but then again rose to 75 after the third part had been published. With the fifth part, however, downloads decreased to around 40.000 and many of those were not paid for. This resulted in King ending his experiment after the sixth part of the serial. He stated that gross income for the six parts of *The Plant* had totaled almost half a million dollars, while his net income after expenses had been exactly $263.832. *The Plant* so far remains unfinished, but the six parts written are nowadays available for free download on King's website.

When King announced that he would take a pause from writing the story but would resume doing it later, he wrote on his website:

Following December's installment of this story--December's very long installment of this story--The Plant will be going back into hibernation so that I can continue work on Black House (the sequel to The Talisman, written in collaboration with Peter Straub). I also need to complete work on two new novels (the first, Dreamcatcher, will be available from Scribner's next March) and see if I can't get going on The Dark Tower again. And my agent insists I need to take a breather so that foreign translation and publication of The Plant--also in installments, also on the Net--can catch up with American publication. Yet don't despair. The last time The Plant furled its leaves, the story remained dormant for nineteen years. If it could survive that, I'm sure it can survive a year or two while I work on other projects.

As I write this, more than 25 years have passed since King decided to pause writing *The Plant*. That pause is still ongoing, and to be honest I believe that King has abandoned his serial for good.

Black Ribbon, a rock opera

In January, 2010, it was announced that Stephen King would contribute to musician and producer Shooter Jennings' dystopian concept album *Black Ribbon*, a rock opera which Jennings conceived of while he travelled across America with his fiancé, actress Drea de Matteo, and their infant daughter Alabama. This was in 2008, and the finance crisis was hitting hard. In their car, they listened to the radio and could hear the fear in people's voices as they imagined disasters to come, from a police state to the end of the United States.

King performs as a fictional radio announcer named Will o' the Wisp, who spends his last hour on the air playing songs by a fictitious band called Hierophant, whose music has been banned by the authorities.

According to Jennings, once he had had the idea of King in the role of Will o' the Wisp, he was unable to imagine anyone else playing that part:

"Once the idea of using him popped in my head, it kind of stayed and never varied. I wrote a script and I sent it to him, and then he took that and he rewrote it and changed it and added quite a lot of great stuff, so at the end of the day, that part of it was a collaboration. He was supportive of what I'd written and liked the voice that I had given the character. I sent it to him and a couple of weeks later, I had a package at my doorstep with a CD, a typed-out transcript and a picture of him doing it."

In another interview, Jennings went into more detail regarding his conviction that King would be perfect for the role:

"He was my first choice. The idea to have a DJ/voice tie the record together came to me much earlier than the concept of the songs. The first thing that struck me was to reach out to Art Bell himself, which I did, but I quickly decided that I needed someone whose voice wasn't so well known and who wouldn't be well known as a talk radio personality. It was going to be a work of fiction and I felt like having a radio personality on the album would take the listener out of the experience."

King liked the idea, and since he also was a fan of Jennings' music, he seems never to have had any doubts about being part of the album:

"It's a tremendously spooky idea. He sent me a draft, and it was just about perfect. I altered a few things and expanded some of it, but he knew exactly what he wanted. To me, it was brilliant, the way the talk and the music weave in and out. I haven't heard the final version, but I heard a rough mix I thought was pretty good, even though I'm not in love with the sound of my own voice."

Interestingly, King and Jennings never met or even talked on the phone during their work on the album. Jennings, who is a fan of King's fiction, sent his proposal via email and King recorded his part in a Florida studio, after which he mailed the digital files to Jennings who incorporated them in his album.

The completed work, named *Black Ribbon*, was released on March 2, 2010. Sadly, it gained little notice, at least among those interested in Stephen King and his work.

The tracks on the album are as follows:

1. "Wake Up!"
2. *"Last Light Radio 11:01 pm" 2:30*
3. "Triskaidekaphobia"

4. "Don't Feed the Animals"
5. "The Breaking Point"
6. *"Last Light Radio 11:16 pm" 1:31*
7. "Everything Else is Illusion"
8. "God Bless Alabama"
9. "All of This Could Have Been Yours"
10. *"Last Light Radio 11:29 pm" 1:11*
11. "Fuck You (I'm Famous)"
12. "Lights in the Sky"
13. "Black Ribbons"
14. *"Last Light Radio 11:40 pm" 1:34*
15. "Summer of Rage"
16. "California via Tennessee"
17. "The Illuminated"
18. *"Last Light Radio 11:57 pm" 1:08*
19. "When the Radio Goes Dead"
20. *"All of This Could Have Been Yours (reprise)" 3:10*

King talks on tracks 2, 6. 10, 14, and 18; on track 20 you hear both King and Jennings.

On the first "Last Light Radio" track, at 11:01, King's character Will o' the Wisp tells us that this is his last night as a radio host before the authorities will seize the station and control its broadcasts. He says that although he usually doesn't play music during his broadcasts, he now intends to do so and will play pieces by a group called Hierophant, which the government has banned.

When Will o' the Wisp returns at 11:16, he talks about how the world has changed. Governments now create disasters and wars in order to then offer solutions and peace, which people gratefully accept. You no longer hear cars or children in the streets, only heavy transports full of armed men. He ends by introducing the next song, "Everything Else Is Illusion", also by Hierophant.

Fourteen minutes later he returns again, and now mentions a book by Carol S. Pearson, *The Hero Within: Six Archetypes We Live By*. It describes the six stages we go through during our lives: The Innocent, The Orphan, The Wanderer, The Warrior, The Martyr, and The Magician. He then introduces another Hierophant song, ”Here's Fuck You (We're Famous)” and recommends his listeners to ”Put all ten middle fingers in the air and dance my brothers and sisters”.

Returning again at 11:40, now in a nostalgic mood, Will o' the Wisp looks back on his ten years of talking to his listeners. At first on a pirate station airing from a disgusting basement room. He talks about a button he owns, with the message ”Killing for peace is like fucking for chastity”. He wishes for hope, but no longer believes anything is left to hope for, not even when numbing himself with liquor. He ends by introducing the Hierophant song ”Summer of Rage”.

In his next to last track, at 11:57, Will o' the Wisp tries to urge his listeners to resist, and fight back.

”We've even won a victory or two for human rights. We said 'Yes we can' and for a while, yes we could. Sometimes we fought the law and the law didn't win.”

Fittingly, he ends by introducing a song called ”When the Radio Goes Dead”.

The final track is short. King is heard only briefly at the beginning av the song ”All of This Could Have Been Yours (reprise)”, when Will o' the Wisp tells us that the military has now entered the station. They gesture to him to turn off his microphone, but he gives them the finger and tells them that he will sign off when he is ready. We then hear a shot, and Will o' the Wisp is silent.

Let's listen to a book

Many of Stephen King's books have been issued as audiobooks, most of them uncut but in a few cases shortened for unknown reasons. Many people like audiobooks, while others don't like them at all. What everyone seems to agree on, however, is that it is important who narrates them. In the case of Stephen King, the names of a handful of narrators immediately come to mind.

One narrator who was often praised and who was also one of the first to be known for narrating King's stories was Frank Muller. He was initially a stage actor in New York City, where he was a member of the Riverside Shakespeare Company, but he became famous primarily for his audiobook work; he won the Audie Award as Best Male Narrator in both 2002 and 2003. Stephen King was of course only one of the authors whose work he read, but his list of King readings is still impressive:

"The Little Sisters of Eluria" (novelette)

Black House (Random House, 2001)

The Dark Tower 1 – The Gunslinger (Donald M. Grant, 1982)

The Dark Tower 2 – The Drawing of the Three (Donald M. Grant, 1987)

The Dark Tower 3 – The Waste Lands (Donald M. Grant, 1991)

The Dark Tower 4 – Wizard and Glass (Donald M. Grant, 1997)

The Green Mile (Signet, 1996)

"The Night Filer" (novelette)

"The Shawshank Redemption" (novelette)

The Talisman (Viking, 1984)

On November 5, 2001, just when Muller was about to leave for a week-long motorcycle journey together with a relative, his wife Erika surprised him by saying that she was pregnant with their second child. After celebrating the happy news Muller and his relative left on their trip. After two hours, Muller lost control of his bike on the freeway after accidentally having glanced off a construction barrel and skidded into a median barrier at around 65 mph. Muller was thrown from his bike and landed headfirst on the concrete pavement. He sustained numerous fractures, lacerations and abrasions, and was taken to Antelope Valley Hospital Medical Center in Lancaster, California, where he went into cardiac arrest three times. He had also suffered severe head trauma, later diagnosed as diffuse axonal injury. Muller never recovered and never again narrated any audiobook. He spent six and a half years in hospital and died June 4, 2008, at Duke University Hospital in Durham, North Carolina:

"We are sad to announce that Frank passed away on Wednesday, June 4, 2008 at Duke University Hospital in Durham, NC. Fortunately, our whole family arrived in time to say goodbye."

Since Muller was unable to work after his accident, Stephen King in 2002 arranged an event in order to raise money for Muller's care and for his family. Together with Pat Conroy, John Grisham, and Peter Straub, King appeared on February 2 at the New York City Town Hall, where the authors all read from their books and asked for contributions.

King then endowed The Wavedancer Foundation, an organization that helps disabled artists, authors and others from the production community, with the proceeds from the fundraising event in the form of a special fund earmarked for Muller. By the end of the evening, almost $250.000 had been donated, and on July 1, 2002, a CD of the authors' readings was released. Peter Straub read an excerpt from *Black House*, John Grisham an excerpt from his novel *The Summons*, and Pat Conroy engaged directly with the audience in a humorous give-and-take on the art of writing. Stephen King read his short story ”The Revenge of Lardass Hogan”.

In addition to Frank Muller, many others have narrated King's stories. Those with the largest number of King titles are Will Patton, Craig Wasson, Ron McLarty, Holter Graham, and George Guidall. But above all, Stephen King himself has kept busy narrating his own work for audiobook publication. Currently, he has narrated the following audiobooks:

Bag of Bones (Scribner, 1998)

The Dark Tower 1 (audio cassette)

The Dark Tower 2 (audio cassette)

The Dark Tower 8: The Wind Through the Keyhole

Elevation (Scribner, 2019)

Fairy Tale (Scribner, 2022)

Needful Things (Viking, 1991)

On Writing (Scribner, 2000)

In addition to those complete books, King has also narrated a number of his shorter stories:

"Bazaar of Bad Dreams" (Scribner, 2015)

"Blood & Smoke" (Scribner, 1999)

"Everything's Eventual" (Scribner, 2002)

"Hearts in Atlantis" (Scribner, 1999)

"Just After Sunset" (Scribner, 2008)

"Nightmares & Dreamscapes" (Viking, 1993)

"Skeleton Crew" (Putnam, 1985)

"You Like it Darker" (Scribner, 2024)

In addition, King also narrated an excerpt from his novel *From a Buick 8* (Scribner, 2002), sent out as part of the marketing of the book.

So what does Stephen King himself think of audiobooks? In an audiobook commercial he says that he listens to from 18 to 24 every year, and also explains his view of the difference between an audiobook and a traditional printed one:

"Audiobooks are important because they come from the oldest tradition of narrative which is oral storytelling. I tell people that the difference between a book that you read and a book that you listen to is like the difference between monophonic sound and surround stereo.

You can't peek ahead. You can't see what's going to happen next you're at the mercy of the reader and that builds suspense."

He also tells us about his own favorite audiobook, and that it was listening to it that made him want Craig Wasson to narrate his own novels.

”I would have to say that the best audio book that I ever listened to was a James Ellroy novel called *Blood's A Rover* (Alfred A. Knopf, 2009). The book was read by a guy named Craig Wasson and when I heard it, I immediately said to myself I want that guy to read some of my books.”

Opinions on whether it is preferable to listen to or read books vary, but personally I like audiobooks. And I like them particularly much when Stephen King narrates his own stories.

An interview with George Guidall

This interview was conducted on November 242, 2003, and *The Dark Tower V: Wolves of the Calla* (Simon & Schuster, 2003) had just been published. George Guidall had recorded his audiobook reading of the novel and was on the verge of beginning to record the two last books in the series. I had the opportunity of talking to him and wondered, among other things, by which means he had managed to give such an excellent reading of the novel.

Lilja: When I read the presentation of you that I got from Simon & Schuster Audio I got to wonder if you ever get any time off. It seems you would have to work constantly to manage to do all those things. How do you find the time?

George Guidall: Time *off*? When you love doing something as much as I love narrating the written word, "time off" is practically a deprivation. After 800 or so unabridged narrations, translating the written art form into the spoken art form becomes a way of life. I record from 9 AM to 4 PM four days a week. That means I'm preparing a book while I'm recording one that I've already read. It's a rhythm I've developed over the years so it's not really as demanding as it may sound. I do always have a book with me, though. If I find myself somewhere with time on my hands and I'm "bookless," I go into a form of withdrawal and read whatever is near. Billboards, discarded newspapers, bumper stickers, even the fine print on credit cards can suffice in an emergency.

Lilja: Of all the things you do, what do you prefer doing? Reading or acting? And why?

George Guidall: I must tell you: After 40 years in the theatre, no activity has as much significance to me or is as satisfying and rewarding as recording a wonderfully written novel. I tour the country with a library presentation entitled *An Evening With George Guidall; The Art And Artifice Of Audiobook Narration.* With every performance I am constantly amazed at the dedication and commitment that audiobook listeners have demonstrated. After a stage performance, people have waited to compliment me and express their appreciation of my work as an actor. These are moments in time, though, and gradually fade in the minds of the audience. Audiobook listeners, however, spend hours of prime time, not only listening, but forming a relationship with the reader on a very primal level. People have always needed to be told stories. They've looked to the story teller for comfort, for escape, for vicarious adventure, and for examples of human potential and achievement that might enrich their lives. Through the grace and talent of some authors I can manage to add to their work a level of emotional immediacy to the reader which makes the book(s) all the more enjoyable. Not better, mind you. Different. Reading Proust is an awesome experience for anyone. *Listening* to it can bring out emotional shades not otherwise appreciated. I've just completed recording Edith Grossman's new translation of *Don Quixote*. What a marvelous journey! Listening to it will make it all the more accessible for people (over 40 hours of ear time!) and add colors that (I hope!) will contribute to the overall appreciation of this wonderful work. And the same with Stephen King's *Dark Tower* series! From *The Gunslinger* to the end of Roland's saga, I hope those who read with their ears get as much enjoyment out of the work as I will have had on completing the last book. Performing the work has opened it up for me, allowed me to highlight relationships, accentuate and perhaps even create moods and take full advantage of Stephen King's imagination. What a pleasure!

Lilja: I couldn't imagine narrating an audio book myself. I wouldn't be able to keep focused for so long. Even though I assume you don't read the whole book in one sitting. I feel it would be hard to keep my voice at the same tone. Do you have any secret tricks?

George Guidall: Secrets? I'm an actor. I've been trained to use MY imagination to bring life to the written word. In the recording studio it's the mind and the voice at work. Too much body work hits the microphone and I have to start over. Don't laugh. It's happened. Sawing the air too much, I've been known to punch the mike and nearly burst an engineer's eardrum. No carbonated beverages. No gas-producing lunches. Dairy is a mucous producer, nuts get in your teeth, coffee dries the mouth, bread is a stomach silencer. But, let's not get too personal. The tricks are vocal. The work is through the mind and heart.

Lilja: How hard is it to get in character when you read a book, and, more interesting, how hard is it to switch between many different characters? My experience is that the narrator's ability to do this can make the difference between success and failure.

George Guidall: Usually, there are about two or three major characters in any novel. Maybe four. The rest are peripheral, important, but not the ones we focus on constantly. There can't be too much vocal play with the main characters. It would draw too much attention away from the flow of the book. One doesn't want the listener to think about the narrator's "wonderful" vocal flexing. There's more room to add color to the other characters, though. One has to have enough differentiation so the listener doesn't spend time trying to figure out who's doing the talking. There are some sadistic authors who have, say, presidential cabinet meetings, or huge family reunions, and when that happens I tend to go slightly psychotic and engineers come into the booth with restraining gear and high-pressure hoses.

Lilja: How do you prepare for recording a book like *Wolves of the Calla*? Do you read the book before you go into the studio?

George Guidall: The most important part of preparation for me is discovering the author's emotional point of view in writing the story. For me, it's not simply a question of conveying information from the page to the ear. One can listen to news broadcasts and get that. There has to be an emotional point of departure at the very outset with which to engage the listener. This is the key for me. I imagine myself as the original story teller and search for an appropriate mood which enables me to tell the story. It's a narrative concept which acts as a frame for the experience. I read every book before we start the recording. It would be unfair to do less. Arrogant, really. The author has spent considerable time creating his piece. I need to do him justice. Would an actor start rehearsals of a play without reading it first? Steven King says, find the truth within the lie. You don't find the emotional truth, or any other kind, by winging it.

Lilja: How long does it take to record a book the size of *Wolves of the Calla*?

George Guidall: The usual ratio is 2:1. One hour of recording for every 2 hours spent doing it. That's an average. Some books are easier. Some more difficult. *Wolves of the Calla* runs approximately 26 hours. That means about 40-50 hours of studio time. Probably less, because I found it engrossing and the prose didn't present any major obstacles. King's writing is honest, with a natural flow of its own. As a literary surfer, I simply rode the wave home. It was great fun.

Lilja: You are picking up after Frank Muller, who read first four *The Dark Tower* books before you. First recording the revised and expanded edition of *The Gunslinger* (Simon & Schuster, 2003), then the three following books. How did this happen and do you feel

Muller's shadow hanging over you? Many fans thought he was *"the"* King reader.

George Guidall: Frank Muller and I have been friends since before I began audiobook narration. We shared the stage in a production of a Georges Feydeau farce entitled *Flea in Her Ear* back in the 1970s. It's a strange feeling recording "his" material. He IS *"the"* King reader, as you say, and it is not my intention to minimize that fact. Actually, recording this material brings me closer to him in a way. I think of him constantly while I do it. It's unavoidable. His tragic accident has deprived many people of extraordinary listening pleasures. Anyone wishing to contribute to his long and arduous recovery can contact the Wavedancer Foundation for information. The funds would be greatly appreciated.

Lilja: It says in your biography that you have recorded over 800 unabridged novels. That is probably more books than I will ever read in my lifetime. Do you have a favorite?

George Guidall: Favorites? There are a few. King's work, of course. Proust's *Swann's Way*, Wally Lamb's *I Know This Much is True*, *Frankenstein*, Thomas H. Cook's mysteries, *Crime and Punishment,* and many more.

Lilja: After reading so many novels by others, haven't you ever thought about writing a novel yourself?

George Guidall: You've probably hit on the reason I love doing this. I'm most likely a frustrated writer. Which is why this interview is so long-winded.

Lilja: Again, thanks for agreeing to the interview. Are there any last thoughts you want to share with the readers of Lilja's Library?

George Guidall: Let us all congratulate Stephen King on his lifetime achievement award at the National Book Awards on November 19th. If anyone deserves it, he certainly does, Not only for his tremendous output, but for his journey to the top as well as his ever-present generosity to fellow writers and, yes, even to audiobook narrators.

Interlude 1: Nozz-A-La

Did you know that Stephen King has invented his own soft drink?

In *The Dark Tower* novels, many of the characters jump repeatedly from one to the other of the different worlds all being centered on the Tower that keeps everything together. At one point, the main characters arrive in a world very similar to our own Keystone World, but not identical. One difference is that a soft drink they have is called Nozz-A-La. But it tastes like Coca-Cola and has a logotype in the same colors as Coca-Cola. This soft drink appears several times throughout the series. At one point, Roland Deschain and his friends are given provisions packed by others, and the basket turns out to contain sandwiches and cans of Nozz-A-La; in a dream, Susanna Dean sees Eddie Dean sporting a shirt printed with ”I DRINK NOZZ-A-LA”.

This soft drink appears also in the television series *Kingdom Hospital* (2004). The manuscript proves that King put it in from the start, and the first time it is show on the screen is when one of the main characters is hit by a car and left in the ditch, where the driver of av van with the Nozz-A-La trademark on its side finds him. But the *Nozz-A-La* logotype in the TV series doesn't look the way it was described in *The Dark Tower* series, most probably because the producers were wary of being sued if their fictional trademark was too similar to Coca-Cola's actual one. The series characters are also shown drinking the beverage, and a vending machine carrying the Nozz-A-La logotype is shown.

Finally, Stephen King also lets his characters drink Nozz-A-La in his short story ”Under the Weather” (in his collection *The Bazaar of Bad Dreams*, Simon & Schuster, 2015). Though it turns out that just as most people call Coca-Cola by its nickname, Coke, Nozz-A-La drinkers also refer to their favorite beverage by a nickname: Nozzy.

As so many of Stephen King's creations, Nozz-A-La has begun to live a life of its own outside of its maker's own work. In the television series *Lost* (running for 121 episodes from 2004 until 2010), a minor character, Henry Gale, arrives at the island in a balloon, on the side of which are listed the companies sponsoring it. One of them is Nozz-A-La. And in Joe Hill's novel *The Fireman* (William Morrow, 2016), some plunderers find Nozz-A-La, among other things.

Should anyone be interested, there are also shirts and can openers with the Nozz-A-La logotype available. But let me mention that Stephen King has had nothing to do with this imaginary merchandise; both have been created by fans of his.

The King of pop and the King of horror create a ghost

"'STEPHEN?...Stephen King?...This is...ummm...Michael? Michael Jackson?' The voice is high, anxious, hopeful, excited, elfin. 'I'm, oh my God, I am such a *fan*!'"

According to Stephen King himself, that was his first conversation with Michael Jackson. It happened in 1993, while King was visiting director Mick Garris during filming of the miniseries made from his novel *The Stand.* King assured Jackson of his reciprocal admiration.

"I'm on the set of *The Stand* miniseries, and out of the blue someone's handed me a phone with the self-anointed King of Pop on the other end of the line."

What Jackson wanted was for King to write the manuscript for his next music video, or as Jackson called it, music film.

"What he wants, it develops, is for me to write the *scariest*, the absolute SCARIEST, music video ever, called *Ghosts*. It will be like the old Frankenstein movies, he explains, only scarier! TERRIFYING! 'Stephen,' he says, 'we *must* do this. We're going to shock the world.'"

King tried to do just that and, as he says, he did it because Michael Jackson asked him to do it, not because he believed that the film would shock its watchers. It is no secret that Stephen King likes to try doing things he has never done before, and writing a miniature musical for Michael Jackson was definitely something new. This is how King describes what Jackson wanted:

"The core story he described to me that day was about a mob of angry townspeople — buttoned-down suburbanites, not torch-carrying peasants — who want the 'weirdo' who lives in the nearby castle to leave town. Because, they say, he's a bad influence on their children."

King interpreted this as a symbol of how music has always been accused of influencing the young, and at the time he knew nothing of the accusations of child abuse that would later be levied at Jackson, though possibly he might have written the film script even if they had been known to him. It is far from uncommon that famous persons are accused of things, ranging from petty theft to the murder of John Lennon, King says, referring to the fact that conspiracy theorist Steve Lightfoot has published both a booklet and a website claiming that King killed Lennon at the behest of then President-elect Ronald Reagan. Lightfoot, of course, stands by his theory even despite the fact that the actual murderer, Mark Chapman, publicly confessed and is still serving his sentence.

The film was initially called "Is This Scary?" and would be directed by Mick Garris. Filming began already in late 1993 and continued for three weeks, but suddenly all work ceased and the project was seemingly dropped. King no longer remembers if he was given any explanation for what had happened (in fact, at this time had Michael Jackson dropped out of the project). What he does remember, however, are some peculiar things involving Michael Jackson that happened.

"One day during preproduction, I was in on a conference call about the choreography, and Michael fell asleep." And at another time, Jackson phoned King's wife, Tabitha, at home: "On another occasion, he called my wife, wanting the phone number for wherever I was that day. She gave it to him. Michael called back five minutes later, on the verge of tears. He hadn't had a pencil, he said, so he'd tried to write the number on the carpet with his finger, and he couldn't read it. My wife gave him the number again. Michael thanked her profusely … but never called me."

Filming of *Ghosts* resumed as suddenly as it had been halted. In his column "The Pop of King" in *Entertainment Weekly* (where it ran from 2003 until 2009) King tells us that in 1996, three years after the events of 1993, Michael Jackson suddenly phoned Mick Garris, exclaiming "Mick, it's gonna happen! We gotta *believe* it's gonna happen!"

And this time *Ghosts* did indeed happen, but with no further involvement from either Stephen King or Mick Garris, who was then working on the miniseries based on King's novel *The Shining* that was broadcast in 1997. By the time the film was made, the manuscript for *Ghosts* had been so extensively rewritten that it can hardly any longer be said to be King's story. But King is not bothered by this; if anything, he is happy that when finally made, the film is as good as it is and that Michael Jackson gets to demonstrate what a fabulous dancer he was.

"The story had wandered a far distance from my original script, but that hardly matters. What does matter is that the video contains some of the best, most inspired dancing of Jackson's career. If you look at it, I think you'll see why Fred Astaire called Jackson 'a helluva mover.'"

An interview with Mick Garris

This interview was done in late 2024 for this book. My intention was to take a closer look at why Mick Garris for a while was the director most often associated with Stephen King adaptions, as well as why that association ended for by now a long while ago. In addition, Garris contributes several interesting anecdotes.

Lilja: You have done more Stephen King film and TV adaptations than any other director. What is it with King's stories that makes you want to adapt them?

Mick Garris: I identify so much with King's outlook on storytelling and life in general. We are very different in many ways, but more alike in even more ways. We were both brought up by single mothers in working class conditions. Though there are a few years between us, we were absorbed by a lot of the same media that we turned to: horror movies, the Universal classics and the junk, as well; books by Matheson and Bradbury and the pulps; television like *The Twilight Zone* and *Outer Limits*. I feel like I live in the worlds that he writes about … and the fact that most of his readers feel that way shows just how universal his voice is.

Lilja: How did you come to work with King? It all started with *Sleepwalkers* in 1992, didn't it?

Mick Garrie: Correct. We were both represented by the CAA talent agency, and my agent at the time, Jon Levin, managed to get me a meeting with the executive in charge of S*leepwalkers* at Columbia Pictures. The meeting went great, they saw quite quickly my passion for and knowledge of King's work, and told me that I would surely get the job. However, they had to meet with another director the next day, as a courtesy to that director's agent, with whom the studio had a relationship.

But … that other director started rewriting the script in a totally different direction from King's screenplay. And if you're going to release a movie called *Stephen King*'s *Sleepwalkers*, it had better resemble what King intended. So … they called me back for another lunch meeting … and afterwards moved me into my director's office! I had no idea they were going to hire me that day, but we started preproduction immediately! They had fired the other director, and asked me to go back to King's original script as much as possible, and address some of the studio notes. So I would call King about their notes, and he would write new pages and fax—yes, fax—them to me. So that's where it began.

Lilja: And then in 1994 you did *The Stand*. That must have been scary both because it's such a huge book to adapt, as well as one of those his readers love most?

Mick Garris: It was scary for a lot of reasons: one, I was the only director for what amounted to four feature films; two, I had never directed anything of a large scope before this; three, it was America's bestselling author's best selling and most beloved book. It was a 460-page script, written by King himself, and had 125 speaking parts, 95 scripted locations, 100 shooting days in six states, and lots and lots of location work, which was constantly beset by every weather condition you can imagine.

Lilja: I guess you have seen the new version. Any comments on that one?

Mick Garris: I was very curious to see something I had made being remade. They went in a very different direction by messing with the timeline, which I found fascinating.

Lilja: Then in 1996 you did the music video *Ghost* with Michael Jackson and in some way, King was involved with that. Can you explain all that? King rarely gets any credit for his involvement with that one.

Mick Garris: Michael had become a huge horror fan after seeing *An American Werewolf in London*, and contacted John Landis to make *Thriller*. Several years later, Michael had signed with Paramount to do the end title song for *Addams Family Values*. *Ghost* started out to be a video for that song. So Michael decided he wanted to make the scariest music video ever ... and if you want something scary, you turn to the writer of the scariest material ever: Stephen King. Michael and King had some conversations, and King wrote a script that was called, at the time, *Is This Scary?*

We were shooting *The Stand* at this time, and King recommended me to Michael to direct. The producers of *The Stand* threatened to fire and sue me if I should dare to take the job during postproduction. But I met with Michael, and we worked it all out. King did the first few drafts of the script, but once things started moving forward, Michael had more and bigger ideas, and I was tasked with all the rewrites.

Working with Michael was wonderful, but there was no structure to Michael's schedule. We shot for two weeks before shutting down when Michael left the country without telling anyone when the first scandal happened. So King was very important to creating the original script and events of the video, but it changed over time. The entire production was shut down for three years before I told Michael that Stan Winston, who was a wonderful director, as well as an amazing makeup and special effects guru and close friend of Michael, should take it over and finish it.

Lilja: Then in 1997 there was a short film *Chattery Teeth* that was part of the collection of three short films with the name *Quicksilver Highway*.

Mick Garris: Yes. We shot that right after shooting *The Shining*, with most of the same crew who had worked on that miniseries. It was a lot of fun, and was shot in my hometown of Los Angeles. It was originally intended to be a pilot for an anthology series at the Fox Network, but it didn't work out that way. I coupled King's story with Clive Barker's short story, and wrote the wraparound segments to make it a movie.

Lilja: And then back to longer adaptations again with *The Shining*. Do you know why King wanted to do that one? Was it just that he didn't like Kubrick's movie version of the book?

Mick Garris: That's pretty much why. After *The Stand* became one of the highest-rated miniseries in television history, the ABC network came to King and asked him what he'd like to do next. And he said *The Shining*. It was a very personal and important book for King, and he always wanted to see a filmed version that was closer to what he had in mind. He wrote the script, and it's one of the best I've ever read.

Lilja: I have read that Kubrick owned the rights to *The Shining* at this time and in order to get the rights to do the TV series King had to agree to stop saying bad things about Kubrick's version. Do you know if there is any truth to that? And if there is, what did King think about that?

Mick Garris: Yes, it's true that part of the deal with Kubrick (who was paid $1.5 million for us to do it) was that King could no longer badmouth the Kubrick film. It was in the contract. I'm sure by 1996 that it was fine with King. He had been very public about his feelings regarding the Kubrick film, and it was no secret what he thought.

Lilja: Do you know if Kubrick ever commented on your version of *The Shining*?

Mick Garris: I never heard. I doubt that he even saw it.

Lilja: If I remember correctly, you once told me that you actually have the hedge animals from *The Shining* saved and placed in your garden. Is that true, and what reactions do you get from people who visit you?

Mick Garris: I have one of the topiary lions right in front of my office, right between my house and my office. It needs a bit of repair and refreshing now and then, which I do regularly. The neighbors love it.

Lilja: King has a cameo in *The Shining,* and if I have understood correctly it's been heavily cut. How come? We King fans love his camos.

Mick Garris: It wasn't because of King! The scene turned into a physical meltdown of all the ghosts at the Overlook Ball, and it suddenly became a zombie movie. We were very careful to pay attention to the human drama of the story, and once in the editing room, it seemed to cheapen the movie a bit. So I decided to take that material out. Which was a really tough decision to make, as King spent at least four hours in makeup preparing for the scene!

Lilja: Then in 2004 you were back with *Riding the Bullet*. The story was originally released as a very early eBook, and is quite short. Was this one easier to adapt? Short story into a feature film?

Mick Garris: Well, easier in one way: the short story was only 30 pages and I had an idea to expand it into something of feature length. Normally, I feel the further away you get from King's source material, the shittier the movie. But this one inspired something really personal to me. I wrote it on spec, and shared my script with Stephen King, who was very supportive of it. So there was a lot of room to add some meat to the bones of King's story, and flesh it out as something that I felt a real kinship to. The backstory of Alan being an art student confronted by death at the age of 21, and the whole idea of death as entertainment, seemed a theme worth approaching. And again, King was very supportive.

Lilja: And in 2006 you directed another TV adaptation, *Desperation.* I get the feeling that you prefer to work with TV rather than feature films when it comes to King. Am I right in that, and, if so, is it just that you get more time or are there other factors?

Mick Garris: Well, my television adaptations have had better budgets than the feature adaptations. I'd love to do feature films over television, because the budgets and censorship issues are usually less of a problem. But the career I've had a has made it possible for me to work as a director on either high-level television or low-to-mid-level features, and given that choice I prefer the former. Also, television requires much more material than feature film markets. But generally you get a lot more time to work on feature films. But yes, if you mean screen time, it is great to be able to tell a whole book in a miniseries or limited series format on television.

Lilja: Were there ever talks about adapting *The Regulators* (Dutton, 1996), *Desperation*'s (Viking, 1996) twin book that was published as written by Richard Bachman? Maybe not back then but today I could see them as two seasons of the same TV series. Same characters but still different.

Mick Garris: *The Regulators* was originally written as a screenplay for Sam Peckinpah, which never got made. So King turned it into a novel. We never spoke about adapting it, though. *Desperation,* ironically, is much more cinematic than *The Regulators*.

Lilja: And then in 2011 you did your (so far) last King adaptation, *Bag of Bones*, and again for TV. How was it to adapt that one? King has mentioned the book as one of his personal favorites. Did that add any pressure on you?

Mick Garris: Well, by that time, I felt I'd earned King's trust. I love the book as well, and he knew that I would put as much passion into this as I do into all of our collaborations. So yes, there's always the pressure of not wanting to fuck it up, but that pressure is usually self-imposed.

Lilja: *Bag of Bones* is a bit special to me because in the promotion for it they produced photos of Pierce Brosnan as the author Mike Noonan and in one there is an ad for a signing he would do at *Lilja's Library*. And they also sent me a fake book that Pierce had signed Mike Noonan's name in.

Mick Garris: That's right!

Lilja: I know it's hard to rate your own stuff, but if you have to pick one of these that you are extra happy with, which one would that be?

Mick Garris: I rarely look back in that way, but it is something I'm often asked. The one that feels most personal is *Riding the Bullet*, which is also one of the least successful things I've ever made. The one that connected with the most people—and one that I've recently seen on the big screen with an audience for the first time—is *The Stand*. I was kind of amazed by how it worked as a film—four films—as opposed to as a television production. It's incredibly complicated in every sense, and technically it was so very, very difficult. It was amazing to see what we were able to achieve under the most difficult of conditions. And *The Shining* had the budget and schedule that allowed me to do some of my most cinematic work. So take your pick!

Lilja: Let's take the opposite tack. If you had the chance to redo one of your King adaptions, which one would that be, and why?

Mick Garris: I don't like looking back. I'm not interested in revisiting something that's already been done. They stand on their own—warts and all—as markers in time. I want to keep moving forward.

Lilja: Since *Bag of Bones* in 2011 you haven't done any more adaptions of Stephen King stories. Is that a conscious decision of yours, or did King feel that it was time for others to get a chance, or did it just happen? Will we see another King adaptation from Mick Garris?

Mick Garris: I have a series that I'm creating that's based on a King story, that is at a network, going through the lawyers for King, the actors, and me, so we'll see what happens there. But there is no greater joy than working with Steve on a project. I don't think anyone said, "well, that's enough of Garris, let's move on", but I'm happy to see Mike Flanagan do such tremendous work with his material. I'm always happy on a set with King!

Lilja: Anything else you'd like to add? Any fun anecdotes from filming any of the movies we haven't heard before?

Mick Garris: Nothing I can think of off the top of my head, Lilja.

Lilja: Thank you so much for taking the time.

Mick Garris: Cheers.

Interlude 2: Zelda

Many actors take part in the films made from Stephen King stories. Some of them are easy to recognize, others may be harder to place. In *Pet Sematary* (1989) there is a character called Zelda Goldman who is the sister of one of the main characters, Rachel Creed. We see her only in retrospective scenes; she lies ill in bed, twisted in spinal meningitis and looking near death. I assume that like myself, most people have always assumed that Zelda was played by some very slim female actress, but the fact is that her role was played by a man, Andrew Hubatsek. So why was a male actor hired to play a woman? Andrew Hubatsek offers a theory in one of the few interviews he has given:

"The only practical reason I can think of is because the makeup took so long, around 14 hours, and required the back and upper chest, face and hands to be glued on by the two makeup artists: this in a very cold trailer in Maine. So I was shirtless for most of the time. Would've been harder for a young woman or girl, modesty wise."

Apart from the considerable makeup demands he also remembers his scenes as challenging. This is how he describes his short but hectic part in the production:

"My experience on the set is a bit of a blur. I got there in the last couple of days of shooting, was put into makeup for at least 14 hours, filmed straight for what seemed like another 18 and then had to be unglued with a solvent for another 6. I was exhausted, sick and in an altered state and I think that might've come out in the film."

Or in other words, Mr. Hubatsek had to put in a huge amount of both work and pain for the those very few minutes he appears in the movie.

A family of authors

Stephen King's family is a family of authors. Claiming anything else is just impossible. King himself, his wife Tabitha, and their two sons Joe and Owen are all writers. The only family member who is not a published author is their daughter Naomi, who instead became a unitarian pastor. Stephen King himself is, obviously, the most productive and well known of them all, but Tabitha King has nevertheless published eight novels as well as short stories and poems; Joseph Hillström King, who publishes under the name "Joe Hill", is publishing his fifth novel in 2025 and has also published three short story collections; Owen King has published three novels – one of them co-written with his father – and one story collection, as well as two published graphic novels with a third forthcoming. But even given that Stephen King had a considerable head start on Joe and Owen, his productivity is staggering – together, Tabitha and her two sons have published twenty books and a number of stories, but this pales in comparison to the almost five times as many books published by Stephen.

But Stephen King doesn't stem from a writing family. His father Donald's last name was actually Pollock, and he changed it to King as an adult. After WW2 he worked as a traveling vacuum salesman. On July 23, 1939, he married Nellie Ruth Pillsbury and they initially lived with Donald's parents. Donald served in the Navy during the war, but after his return they moved to Scarborough, a small town about six miles south of Portland, Maine. During their first several years of marriage they came to believe themselves unable to have children, and so adopted David (September 14, 1945 – June 5, 2021); when Stephen was born in 1947, he came as a surprise to his parents.

When Stephen King was four, in 1951, his father Donald left his family. King never meet him again, and he died in 1980, 66 years old. When asked if he would have liked to meet his father, King has replied:

"No. I was curious when I was a kid. I used to think, 'I'd like to find him and knock his fucking head off.' And then later on, I thought to myself, 'I'd like to find him and hear his side of the story and then knock his fucking head off.'"

But King never tried to find his father, who turned out to have lived in a small town in Pennsylvania, Wind Gap, with a new family.

In an interview published in *Rolling Stone*, King was asked whether his father's early disappearance has affected him, and replied by telling of his proposal to Tabitha. Anyone who expects it to have been a romantic moment will have to think again.

"I can remember when Tabby and I got married, back in '71. I can remember laying in bed with her and turning over and saying, 'We ought to get married.' And she said, 'Let me think about it overnight.' And in the morning, she said, 'Yeah, we should get married.'"

Despite having very limited means, they married on January 2, 1971. King has said that they basically had no money. He worked at Wet-Wash Laundry while Tabitha had a job in a Dunkin' Donuts outlet.

"We must have been fucking crazy. She would go to work at Dunkin' Donuts. She looked cute in the little pink uniform. God, she was so good-looking. She's still good-looking to me, but oh, my God. And there was something sexy about all that pink nylon."

When the King's oldest son Joseph decided to start writing, he wanted to be certain that his work was published because of its merit, not just because he was the son of one of the world's most popular authors. For this reason, he shortened his first and middle names by half and got rid of his family name; Joseph Hillström King became Joe Hill.

"I really wanted to allow myself to rise and fall on my own merits. One of the good things about it was that it let me make my mistakes in private."

Hill had learned early on that having King as a family name could be both an advantage and a disadvantage. When he was twelve years old, Bangor *Daily News* published an essay of his.

"I was completely pumped. I felt like I was on the verge of major celebrity, and my excitement about the piece lasted right up until the day it was published. When I read it in the newspaper, I realized for the first time that it was full of trite ideas and windy writing. At the end, they had added a little postscript that said, 'Joseph King is the son of best-selling novelist Stephen King,' and when I read that I knew that was the only reason they published the piece."

He didn't chose his new name just because it was easy to derive from his legal name, but also as a tribute to the historical Joe Hill (1879–1915), after whom he was named – that Joe Hill's actual name was Joel Emmanuel Hägglund, but as a trade unionist he used "Joseph Hillström" as a pseudonym, and for his songs, cartoons, and other writings he shortened that name to "Joe Hill". He was convicted on dubious evidence for murder and executed in Salt Lake City on November 19, 1915; later his fame grew, and he became a figurehead for the IWW unionists. Both Stephen and Tabitha King came of age in the 1960s, and "were both pretty feisty liberals and looked at Joe Hill as a heroic figure", according to their son Joe Hill.

Hill managed to be accepted by a literary agent, Mickey Choate, in the same way any other aspiring author – by submitting his writings – and without telling him of his parents; Choate didn't learn who Joe Hill's father was until eight years after having accepted him as a client. Hill's early experience with publishers was uniformly negative. The first longer work he submitted was an epic fantasy novel, inspired by both J.R.R. Tolkien and John Irving but expressing mainly the values of Irving. It is a story of child raising in an imaginary world. After the book had been rejected by every publisher it had been submitted to, Hill seriously considered resubmitting it under his real name, since he honestly thought it worth publishing:

"After that, maybe there was some feeling like, uh, you know, maybe you should. ... But I actually kind of wound up feeling like the pen name had done its job. If it wasn't good enough to get accepted on its own merits, then that was a healthy thing."

Ultimately, Hill decided that his new name made him free to write in his own way, while a novel by "Joseph King" probably would tend more towards horror. He began selling short stories in the last half of the 1990s, and his first book was a collection of stories called *20th Century Ghosts* (PS Publishing, 2005). When at last he sold a novel to a major publisher (*Heart-Shaped Box* was published by William Morrow in 2007), he felt that his real identity would probably be disclosed, so after signing his contract he told his editor, Jennifer Brehl, both his real name and the identity of his father. Brehl agreed that the book would be published under the Joe Hill name, and that his relationship to Stephen King would not be discussed. But there was hardly any was to keep it secret.

"I had pretty much run to the end of my rope around that time. I had done an appearance in England, and people kind of noticed a little bit of a family resemblance. There started to be some muttering going around. It would have been nice if the book could have come out and been out for a while, but it just didn't work out that way."

Since his relation to Stephen King became public knowledge in 2007, Joe Hill's career has continued, and he has published a further four novels as well as more both stories and collections. He has also written the manuscripts to a number of comics and graphic novels, the best know of them being *Locke & Key*, which has also been adopted as a Netflix series. Even though Joe Hill's style is influenced by his father's, he seems not to have inherited his productivity – since his first published novel (*Carrie*, in 1974), Stephen King has until Spring, 2025, followed it with a further 89 books, which comes to just about one and three quarters of a second book per year. None of the other writers in his family is even close to this record.

Joe Hill and Stephen King have published few collaborations, and those only short stories. their first story together was ”Throttle”, written for an anthology edited by Christopher Conlon to honor author Richard Matheson, *He Is Legend* (Gauntlet Press, 2009); their story is a variation on Matheson's classic ”Duel” from 1971. Three years later they wrote ”In the Tall Grass”, which was serialized in the June and July 2012 issues of *Esquire*; it was turned into a Netflix film in 2019.

As for the other family writers, Stephen King has never published anything in collaboration with his wife Tabitha King, but with his younger son Owen he has written a novel *Sleeping Beauties* (Simon & Schuster, 2017). Stephen and Owen King both have markedly personal writing styles, which made the book quite different from what either has published on his own, and this led to the book receiving very mixed reactions. A graphic novel from the book has already been published, and a TV series is planned.

An interview with Joe Hill

Joe Hill is Stephen and Tabitha King's oldest son and his writing style is more similar to his father's than is that of his younger brother Owen. I personally always recommend readers who like Stephen King to also try Joe Hill's; if you like one of them, you will probably also like the other. On May 20, 2019, I had the opportunity of talking to Joe Hill in connection with the premiere of the TV serial adapted from his novel *NOS4A2* (William Morrow, 2013). The interview was conducted by e-mail and touches on several interesting subjects, both regarding Hill's opinion on transforming a novel into film, and on his then current projects.

The first thing I ask Joe when we begin talking is how he came up with the title *NOS4A2* (which I think is brilliant). He tells me how in the 1980's he, like a lot of us, played arcade games and when and if you were good enough to get on the high score list you could only use five or six letters to enter your name. That is where he first saw the name NOS4A2. So, if you played arcade games in or close to the Bangor area and used that name, chances are that you were part of the inspiration for Joe's book.

NOS4A2 is about Charlie Manx (played by Zachary Quinto in the TV series) who abducts children he considers to be maltreated by their parents. "The parents aren't bad people, they are just regular people," Joe explains, "but Manx sees himself as the hero in his own story when he brings the children to Christmasland where it's against the law to be sad." Manx is very old and his take on women and children is just as old and outdated. He has huge problems with strong women and here both Vic McQueen (played by Ashleigh Cummings) and her friend Maggie Leigh (played by Jahkara Smith) are women whom Manx could never accept. On the whole Manx is a very complex character. We see him getting furious when someone grabs a child by the arm, since he thinks they mistreat them; then he uses them as fuel for his Rolls-Royce Wraith until there is nothing left of them … except teeth.

I have seen the first six episodes of the show and I'm very impressed. The story, although it has been somewhat changed compared to the book, is there. The look of the show is great and I love the actors. Both Zachary Quinto and Ashleigh Cummings are great and they really bring Manx and Vic out of the book and on to the screen. But the one that impresses me the most is the Icelandic actor Olafur Darri Olafsson who plays Bing Partridge. "Bing is Manx ultimate victim," Joe says. "He loves Christmas and has memories from Christmas."

Before the interview was over I got a chance to ask about the future and besides *NOS4A2* that premiers on AMC on June 2nd we have a lot to look forward to. In October the adaptation of "In The Tall Grass" (that Joe wrote with his father) will air on Netflix and he has a collection called *Full Throttle* (William Morrow, 2019) released the same month. The book contains 13 stories of which two are completely new: "Late Returns", which is about a librarian who lends out books to dead people, and "Mums". We also get the two stories he collaborated on with his dad, "In The Tall Grass" and "Throttle", as well as "By the Silvery Waters of Lake Champlain" that's being filmed for the TV series *Creepshow* on Shudder. Then in the spring we get to see Locke & Key (2011) on Netflix.

But that isn't all. Joe is also working on two new books. One is a 200-something pages long book called *Up The Chimney Down* that's currently on the back burner. The other one he doesn't want to reveal anything about, not even the title, but one thing is clear: we'll be seeing a lot more from Joe Hill in the future.

Som fifteen months later I again had the opportunity of talking with Joe Hill. This time the occasion was the premiere of the second season of *NOS4A2.* But we also talked about his role on social media, about a book he has abandoned and about one he hoped to have published in 2022. Unfortunately, however, it has later been delayed and will now be published in late fall, 2025, and retitled *King Sorrow* (William Morrow, 2025).

This interview was booked for August 24, 2020, and as is often the case when time for an interview is set up in advance, you either keep that time or forget about the interview. In this case, I happened to be invited to friends, but problems are there for us to solve. So I excused myself for a short while during the party, went out and simply did the interview sitting in my car in the yard outside the house of our hosts for the evening.

So here I am, sitting in my car and phoning Joe Hill.

Joe Hill: Hi Hans, how are you? Good to talk to you.

Lilja: Yeah, same here. Thanks for taking the time.

Joe Hill: It's a pleasure.

Lilja: I've seen the second season of *NOS4A2*, liked it, but also thought it followed the book more closely than the first season did.

Joe Hill: Yeah, I think there is some truth to that.

Lilja: Season one was almost like a prequel to the book, and then the book happened in season two. Is that how you see it as well?

Joe Hill: Well, I don't know if I would say that the first season is a prequel to the book. I would say it expands on the first third of the book to tell us more about these characters and show us more of their inner lives but I do think that the first season of *NOS4A2* is like the *Terminator* (1984) and the second season is more like *Terminator 2* (1991). In the first season we introduce the world and we're learning about who these people are and sort of setting up the rules and expectations but then in the second season we get to hammer down from the first episode. We're going from 70 miles per hour to 120 miles per hour as fast as we can and for storytelling that's where I'm the most comfortable. I've done a lot of writing for comic books, and I have a comic book imagination, so it's my feeling that stories work best when characters are imperiled. It doesn't need to be physical. Moral, emotional or spiritual can be very powerful, but if there is no sense of danger or risk you might be in trouble. You might not even have a story at all.

Lilja: Yeah, I agree. Do you think we'll see a third season of *NOS4A2*?

Joe Hill: I think we could. I'm really happy with the show. I adore Jami O'Brien, the showrunner, and her lieutenant Tom Brady and their entire talented writers' room. I'm in admiration of the work the actors have done all across the boards from the bigger parts like Ashleigh Cummings to smaller roles. Vic and Linda played by Virginia Kull delivers some of the most emotionally hard-hitting stuff in the second season, so we have been very lucky. I feel that if we only get two seasons, we can go out with our heads held high, we told the story we wanted to tell, to the best of our ability. But could there be more? I think that depends on the viewers. In the second season we begin to introduce new characters like The Hourglass man and old Snake who have supernatural powers of their own much like Charlie and Vic McQueen, and there are a lot of strong creatives in the world of *NOS4A2*, some of them good and some of them very, very bad. There are certainly more to explore there if there is an appetite for it.

Lilja: Yeah, I would definitely like to see a third season with more villains like The Hourglass man.

Joe Hill: [laugh]

Lilja: I really enjoyed him and was actually sad to see him go.

Joe Hill: Oh yeah, the poor Hourglass. He was a real sinister figure and I think we can all breathe easier since he is definitely, certainly, 100 per cent absolutely dead.

Lilja: You also have the TV series *Locke & Key* on Netflix, and it's kind of different how we can see a TV series now from how we watched ten years ago. Some release all episodes at once and others one episode a week. Do you have a preferred way you like to watch a show?

Joe Hill: This is interesting. To talk about this subject I need to be a bit of a film business geek, but here is the thing. At the risk of sounding like a film business nerd there are two ways to deliver a television show. Streaming as on platforms like Netflix and Hulu has been growing in popularity for the last decade, while the other way to deliver a television show is by linear television, which basically means TV on a schedule, that is: a show airs at a particular time. Now the narrative in Hollywood is that linear television is on the way out and that streaming is definitely the future. I definitely think there's room for both and I love Netflix as much as the next guy, the storytelling they do is amazing, but it's interesting that in the time of the coronavirus linear television suddenly looks good. Every Sunday night when a new episode of *NOS4A2* aired, the *NOS4A2* hashtag on Twitter turned into a kind of party with people commenting on what's happening on the show in real time and having a conversation about it. These days no one can go to the movie theaters because of the risks to one's health, and then this is the next best thing, being able to sit at home, and enjoy a scary story together using while connected via the Internet. There is a lot to hate about social media, but this is one part of social media that is very cool.

Lilja: Yeah, it's good when everyone is on the same episode and you can't spoil it.

Joe Hill: And the thing with streaming a show is that you can watch when it fits your schedule, which is great, just click a button and it's on right away … but … when you are watching something linear you're all discovering it at the same time and I think in an era when people are socially distancing, when you can't go to restaurants or movie theatres and you can't socialize the way you used to, this is one way to bridge the gap and I think that horror is especially, and this is going to sound strange, but I think horror is especially good at bringing people together. People love sharing the experience of being scared. That is why it's more fun to ride a rollercoaster that's packed than one with just one or two people. You want to hear everyone else screaming, it makes it more fun.

Lilja: You mentioned social media. I know you are quite active on Twitter...

Joe Hill: I'm sorry to hear you say that [laugh]. I'm trying to shrink my profile on Twitter. I try to spend less time there because I don't think it's a healthy place.

Lilja: But it's a good way to reach a lot of people for good discussions, right? There will always be bad ones as well, but still ...

Joe Hill: I recently re-read *Nineteen Eighty-Four* (Secker and Warburg, 1949) since I wrote an introduction for a limited edition from Suntup Editions, and when you look at social media … to me when you look at *Nineteen Eighty-Four* they all turn in on the same time, hating whoever is on the screen, screaming at them, throwing things at the monitor and to me that is not how I want to be as a human being. I don't want to engage in tribal hate and I see a lot of that on social media, and sometime it's sort of justified, but the thing is that most people have stupid ideas and do stupid things and really intelligent wonderful people can be totally clueless and upsetting in some aspects of their lives, but on social media your stupid moments are recorded forever and you can be declared a kind of unperson for screwing up and I don't think that is the right way to respond to people. Hatred is not the right way to respond to other people's screwups.

Lilja: I see what you mean.

You are very busy working on TV shows and books and comics. Have you been even more productive now with the isolation?

Joe Hill: It's about the same, I'm trying to slow down a little bit but I had a really busy year last year when I was writing four comic books at once plus working on the beginning of a novel, and I was writing screenplays as well. I made it through and I think I did good work and I'm pretty happy with what I came out with, but by the end of the year I thought "I can't keep up this pace, I have to slow down. This isn't healthy to pile up work like this". So right now, I've turned down the volume on work a bit, I'm working on a novel, I'm generally writing one comic book on the side as well, but I won't work on more than one comic book at a time. Carrying five comic books at the same time was cool to try but I don't think I can keep going like that for year after year.

Lilja: Yeah, I understand.

Joe Hill: Some people can, though. Some of the writers I admire the most can carry four or five comic books at the same time. In some way I think of myself more as a comic book writer than a novelist, and to a lot of my peers it's a routine to carry four or five comic books at the same time.

Lilja: Can we expect a new book this year, or will we have to wait until next?

Joe Hill: The next book might be out in the spring of 2022. I have one I'm working on. I'm really happy with it and it's really tugging along, but I'm not talking about it too much. It's another really big one like *The Fireman* (William Morrow, 2016) and *NOS4A2,* and I think realistically at the pace it's going, given some of the slowdowns associated with the Corona virus and the economic setback, probably not another novel next year, probably not until 2022.

Lilja: When we spoke last year when season one of *NOS4A2* aired, you mentioned that you were working on a book called *Up the Chimney Down*. Is that something you're still working on?

Joe Hill: I got two hundred pages of *Up the Chimney Down* and I think it's a pretty good book, but I'm not working on it at the moment. And sometimes though, to bring it back to *NOS4A2* for a minute. At one point I had Charlies backstory, the story of his childhood and how he got his supernatural gifts. Originally that was part of the novel but it slowed the action down when we wanted to go faster and later I reinvented that material as a graphic novel in a comic book called *Wraith* and we got to tell Charlies back story in a more satisfying way and probably the most exciting exploration of Charlie's youth and powers are in the TV show. I have thought lately about *Up the Chimney Down* and wondered if it's actually a comic book instead. So, I don't feel it was wasted effort and I don't think it's a failed book, it's just sort of a thing I'm still kind of looking at, thinking about, trying to decide what its best final shape is. And this is not uncommon. I had a lot of this with *Horns*. I had a long time with it where it went through different forms, different titles, different characters, before I finally settled on the story I wanted to tell. So, I can wait [laugh].

Lilja: Speaking of *NOS4A2,* do you think you'll write more about Charlie Manx in novel form?

Joe Hill: Well, I definitely think there is room for the TV show to continue if there is an appetite for it. Within the book I mentioned a couple of things. At one point we get this map of United Inscapes of North America and there is a place on that map, it's full of imaginary locations and one of those places is a town called Orphanhenge, and I have had a story idea for Orphanhenge for years. Whether I'm going to write it is another question, but it's something I've thought about. You know most of my dad's stories seems to take place in the same universe so *Cujo* (Viking, 1981) takes place in the same world as *The Dead Zone* (Viking 1979) and all the worlds are united by *The Dark Tower* (Grant, 1982) and in some ways I think that a lot of my stories are all taking place in the same world and maybe that world is one level down in the tower from the worlds of my dad's stories. So, I think the answer to if there will be more to this world is probably kind of inevitable, because that is the world where my imaginations comes from, that's the world where all the stories come from, that same fabric.

Lilja: You mentioned your dad's books. A lot of people online have been speculating about if *NOS4A2* is connected to his books and if it is set in the same universe. And on the map you mentioned we can also find the Pennywise Circus, so is there any truth to that?

Joe Hill: Yeah, you know I thought that when I did Stephen King references it was a joke … at first. I always thought they were jokes and that there wasn't anything deeper to them. At one point when I was working on *The Fireman* I did begin to imagine that maybe the world of my story is somewhat adjacent to the world of his in a more curious way which would make sense because I'm somewhat adjacent to him because Tabitha and he raised me and the context of my life is my parents' work and having them in my life as mentors, and they are the people that care about me so I think invariably there is some connection in my stories to his and in my stories to my mom's as well.

Lilja: Makes total sense.

Thanks for taking the time to talk to me and I look forward to seeing what's next for you.

Creating while under the influence

There has been a lot of things said and written about Stephen King having been an alcohol and drug abuser. Some people claim that it affects his writing, some that it is noticeable only in certain stories and that they can see exactly in which. Others claim that it hasn't had any effect at all om King's work. I suspect that the truth is somewhere in between those claims.

According to King himself, he started drinking at the age of eighteen, which in his case meant the mid-1960s. He has also stated that he began using cocaine in 1978, at the time he realized that his drinking had become problematic. In a *Rolling Stone* interview in 2014 he spoke of accepting that he was an alcoholic:

"I realized I had a problem around the time that Maine became the first state in the nation to pass a returnable-bottle-and-can law. You could no longer just toss the shit away, you saved it, and you turned it in to a recycling center. And nobody in the house drank but me. My wife would have a glass of wine and that was all. So I went in the garage one night, and the trash can that was set aside for beer cans was full to the top. It had been empty the week before. I was drinking, like, a case of beer a night. And I thought, 'I'm an alcoholic.' That was probably about '78, '79. I thought, 'I've gotta be really careful, because if somebody says, 'You're drinking too much, you have to quit,' I won't be able to."

At this time King worked on new writings during the mornings while editing his ongoing work in the evenings, and it was mainly in the evenings he drank. Perhaps this was what saved his work from crashing entirely. Because in truth King was under the influence of alcohol during at least part of his work on all of his first 26 books;

while writing the last twenty of those books, cocaine also played a large part in his life.

"Coke was different from booze. Booze, I could wait, and I didn't drink or anything. But I used coke all the time."

So how did King manage to write bestsellers and be a good husband and father of three while at the same time being an addict? In the *Rolling Stone* interview, he says that he simply can't remember.

"That whole time is pretty hazy to me. I just didn't use it around people. And I wasn't a social drinker. I used to say that I didn't want to go to bars because they were full of assholes like me."

You may find this hard to believe, and in fact King himself agrees with you.

"Well, I can't comprehend it now, either, but you do what you have to do. And when you're an addict, you have to use. So you just try to balance things out as best you can. But little by little, the family life started to show cracks. I was usually pretty good about it. I was able to get up and make the kids breakfast and get them off to school. And I was strong; I had a lot of energy. I would've killed myself otherwise. But the books start to show it after a while. *Misery* (Viking, 1987) is a book about cocaine. Annie Wilkes is cocaine. She was my number-one fan."

Misery (Viking, 1987) is not the only one of King's novels that bear witness to his addiction. Already *The Shining* (Doubleday, 1977) can be read as a cry for help. King also claims that he has no memories of editing either *Cujo* or *The Tommyknockers* (Putnam, 1987).

"*The Tommyknockers* is an awful book. That was the last one I wrote before I cleaned up my act. There's really a good book in here, underneath all the sort of spurious energy that cocaine provides, and I ought to go back. The book is about 700 pages long, and I'm thinking, 'There's probably a good 350-page novel in there'."

Even if King sobered up in 1986 *Tommyknockers* is by no means the only one of his books that he feels demonstrates how bad a novel written by an addict can turn out to be.

"I don't like *Dreamcatcher* (Simon & Schuster, 2001) very much. *Dreamcatcher* was written after the accident. I was using a lot of Oxycontin for pain. And I couldn't work on a computer back then because it hurt too much to sit in that position. So I wrote the whole thing longhand. And I was pretty stoned when I wrote it, because of the Oxy, and that's another book that shows the drugs at work."

The accident King mentions occurred on June 19, 1999, when he was out walking and was hit by a truck driven by Bryan Smith.

This said, I doubt that readers are actually able to see that King wrote under the influence of alcohol and cocaine. Certainly some novels stand out as different from the others, or as more odd; some may even be less satisfying than others, but remember that according to Stephen King himself we are talking about at least the first 26 of his by now 90 books. In hindsight, it is of course easy to blame weaknesses in some of them on the influence of drugs. But remember that among the novels published during those first years we also find titles like *Carrie*, *The Shining*, *The Stand*, *It* and *Pet Sematary*. Should we attribute their qualities as well to the influence of addiction?

The Thing of Evil – Stephen King vs. social media

The Thing of Evil. Is it a horror movie? Yet another epithet for Sauron or for Satan? Not at all. It is the pet name given by Stephen King to his dog Molly. In fact a very cute dog.

The first photo of Molly appeared on December 16, 2014. King put it up on his Twitter (now X) account, where he introduced Molly as the newest member of the King family – a Corgi puppy. In that first image we saw her chewing on a Santa hat, and King's comment read, "My new puppy chews up a Santa hat. Good idea."

Since then, Molly has been present in King's media comments. Usually photographed in funny situations and always with some fitting comment by King. Among other things we have learned of Molly is that she plans to conquer the world, that she intends taking over running the King household, that she takes selfies which she forces King to publish, and that she celebrates her birthday. In a film snippet we see her in a tug of war with Uncle McMurtry, Joe Hill's Corgi and named for author Larry McMurtry. Here are a few of Stephen King's postings on Molly:

"Molly, aka the Thing of Evil, considers unleashing her battalion of zombie Irish Wolfhounds on Vermont."

"Molly, aka the Thing of Evil, has taken a paws-on selfie for all her Twitter fans, and forced me to post it. Or else."

"Molly, aka the Thing of Evil, celebrates her first birthday. Her plans for Year Two are, well, unspeakable."

"Molly, aka the Thing of Evil, hides from the FBI after stealing the mailman's bag of dog biscuits. Federal crime."

Like all dog lovers, King likes to photograph and film Molly, but sometimes he is a bit too hasty when uploading his pictures. On a few occasions he has published photographs where Molly's collar is clearly visible, which means that the phone number to her owners was also legible. This was hardly appreciated by King's staff, and they most probably pointed it out to him before the images were quickly removed.

In 2018, Molly was a cover girl on *Beachcomber* magazine, since she was that issue's "pet", and in 2021 King wrote an introduction to Zoey Acoff's *The Little Book of Big Corgi Butts* (Harry N. Abrams, 2021), a humorous but endearing book for Corgi lovers. In the summer of 2023, we could follow events after the veterinarian had found a tumor in Molly's neck. She had an operation to remove it, and thankfully the tumor turned out to be benign. Molly quickly recuperated and went back to, as The Thing of Evil does, murder her stuffed animals.

Many of us would love to see a book about Molly. So far, King hasn't written one, but perhaps at some point there will be a *Molly, The Thing of Evil: A Biography*. And who knows, if that happens perhaps we will learn more about King's love for Corgis, which started when his brother in law in the early 1980s acquired a dog named Jimmy.

In an interview published in *Welsh Corgi News*, King says that the first Corgi in the King family was named Bill, suffered from epilepsy and lived for only three years. After that, Tabitha got Vixen, known as The Thing of Good. Vixen (who died in 2018) inspired King to write his short story "Laurie" (included in *You Like It Darker*), and he also dedicated his story to her by adding the words, "Thinking of Vixen". Vixen loved Tabitha above everything else, slept in her bed and was devastated when Tabitha left the house. King realized that he, too, wanted a dog who loved him in the same way, and this was how Molly entered his life.

Twitter (now X) was not King's first attempt at social media. On January 13, 2013, his first official presence of Facebook was added. This was a public Facebook-profile where Stephen King himself was not personally involved, but as a source of news it was highly appreciated:

"The Official Facebook Page for International Best Selling Author Stephen King. Please Note: This page is managed by StephenKing.com (The Official Web Site). Stephen does not contribute directly to the content on this page."

At some point between 2013 and 2015 King then created a personal account. In 2013 he also appeared on both Twitter and Instagram King's first posting on Twitter appeared on December 6, 2013, and his first on Bluesky on November 5, 2023:

"Hello world, Steve King here. Happy 2B here."

Already in 2020, however, King began curtailing his presence on social media. On February 1, 2020, he shut both down his Facebook page and left Instagram, writing

"I'm quitting Facebook. Not comfortable with the flood of false information that's allowed in its political advertising, nor am I confident in its ability to protect its users' privacy. Follow me (and Molly, aka The Thing of Evil) on Twitter, if you like."

Next was X (previously Twitter), which King left after Donald Trump's victory in the November, 2024, Presidential election. On November 14, at 9:57 PM, he wrote a last posting:

“I’m leaving Twitter. Tried to stay, but the atmosphere has just become too toxic. Follow me on Threads, if you like.”

From there, he moved on to Threads, the social media service run by Instagram, fairly similar to X. He began by posting a brief note on Trump:

”Trump’s cabinet picks are ludicrous. The Klown Kar isn’t absolutely full, but it’s getting there.”

In a third posting, also on November 14, he explained why he had left X:

”I quit Twitter. Eleven years, man. It really changed. Grew dark.”

In his sixth and eleventh postings (November 15 and November 18) he went on to praise Threads:

“Being here on Threads feels freeing”

“I’m a Threads guy now.”

As of this writing, King is active only on Threads and Bluesky, though he began posting their only in 2024 after a fairly long break. On June 14, he wrote,

”It’s Flag Day. Randall Flagg day.”

For now, he has alternated between writing on X, Threads and on Bluesky. It remains to be seen for how long he does, and if indeed he stays on those platforms.

Interlude 3: The eBook

On February 22, 2000, Stephen King's US publisher, Simon & Schuster, sent out a press release stating that on March 14, King would release his first eBook, *Riding the Bullet* (Simon & Schuster, 2000). Later in the same year, King also released the first part of his unfinished serial *The Plant* as an eBook for download via his own home page, but *Riding the Bullet* was first.

The booklet was released for downloading at 12:01 AM, Eastern standard time, or in other words one minute after midnight on March 14. It cost $2.50 and was actually a short story of 16,000 words. So the cost was negligible to most readers, but there was another problem. You had to pay for the download via a cash or credit card, which far from everyone had at the time, while many of those who did were afraid to use it online. Everyone had heard horror stories of how easily your card information could be hijacked on the Internet, after which you would lose everything in you accounts in no time.

None of that was true, of course. But what was true was that a few individuals within hours after the release managed to crack the safety code on the file, and began handing the eBook out free of charge.

"Ur" – a new publishing format

If Stephen King enthusiasts wish for anything, it really is to read everything new he writes as soon as possible. Waiting for it is definitely not our thing. So many of us were shocked to the bone when Amazon announced that King had written a story for the company which would be available only on its new eBook reader, Kindle.

Amazon made the announcement of their exclusive publication of "Ur" in early February, 2009:

Author Stephen King announced today that he is releasing a novella, Ur, which will only be available on Kindle. Ur is available for pre-order beginning today and will be released later this month.

And the story itself was described in this way:

In his new novella, Ur, King is at his unsettling best as he examines the future of the written word - for better or worse. Following a nasty break-up, lovelorn college English instructor Wesley Smith can't seem to get his ex-girlfriend's parting shot out of his head: 'Why can't you just read off the computer like the rest of us?' Egged on by her question and piqued by a student's suggestion, Wesley places an order for Amazon.com's Kindle eReader. The [pink?] device that arrives in a box stamped with the smile logo – via one-day delivery that he hadn't requested – unlocks a literary world that even the most avid of book lovers could never imagine. But once the door is open, there are those things that one hopes we'll never read or live through.

In general, Stephen King has hardly been viewed as someone who immediately embraces new technologies, but in this case he seemed to like what he saw. He describes the new Kindle (version 2) as a pretty neat gizmo and says that those who have created it obviously has learned from what didn't work in the first version, something that suggests that he had experimented even with that earlier version.

In an interview published in *USA Today*, however, it seems clear that King is more interested in how his story will be received by readers than in the technical aspects of how it will reach them. Edward C. Baig asks King whether it is important by what means a story reaches its audience:

"The delivery mechanism to my mind is secondary for me as a writer. That isn't necessarily true for people in the business end of it. But I did this once before with a story called *Riding the Bullet* and I never had so many guys in suits come up to me and ask me questions. But they didn't want to know about the story, they didn't want to know about the process, they wanted to know about the delivery system, but to me that's secondary."

Nor does King think that the new technology changes his way of communicating with readers:

"No not really. It might if I were living hand to mouth but I'm one of the fortunate few people who could write pretty much what I want."

So what happened to all of us who wanted to read "Ur" as soon as possible?

On February 10, 2009, we were informed that "Ur" would be released exclusively for Amazon Kindle 2. Everyone else would have to wait from one to three months. On February 12 it was released for Kindle and already four days later, February 16, it was released as an audiobook read by Holter Graham. From March 4 you could download a Kindle app to iPhone, making it possible to read the story on you mobile, and December 30 another app made it possible to read the story on your computer. During a public appearance in Florida on January 29, 1915, King confirmed that "Ur" would be included in his next story collection, *The Bazaar of the Bizarre* (Simon § Schuster, 1015), which was published on November 3.

The story was positively received, but never became quite the success you can call King's earlier eBook experiment with "Riding the Bullet". "Ur" was downloaded several hundred thousand times. On March 3, 2006, King via his literary agent Ralph Vicinanza made this statement regarding sales of the story:

"We've been told that they're in the five figures already. We're excited. They're happy, we're happy and from the initial information that we're getting it seems to be a success."

But "five figures" means less than 100,000 downloads. Vicinanza also said that he had been the one to suggest to King to write and publish the story only as an eBook, in spite of eBooks at this time accounting for only one per cent of total book sales. He had wanted King to do it in order to "create some excitement" for electronic publishing at a time when the publishing industry as a whole was going through a tough period.

Some readers accused King of having sold out and engaging in product placement, but Vicinanza strongly denied that:

"King fans recognize how often cars and other products appear in his books. There isn't enough money out there for Stephen King to do product placement, for sure."

But in spite of Vicinanza's claim, he must have realized that there definitely was a difference between naming a certain brand of car in a novel, and publishing a story in only one specific reading device.

Stephen King had begun writing ”Ur” on January 18, 2009. His editor had read the story and sent it to Amazon by February 4. The final proof was returned to King and his agent, on their Kindles, two days later, February 6. Just as he says in one of his mottos, ”IT’S THE STORY NOT THE TELLER,THAT IS IMPORTANT”, it seems clear that Stephen King views Kindle as a story delivery system. But to him it is still the story itself that is the important thing.

The dedications of Stephen King – to whom, and why

That authors dedicate their books to someone is hardly unusual – there are examples from as early as classical Athens and Rome, and in modern times it has become an almost universal practice. (Even I have dedicated this book to my children.) But sometimes it can be difficult for outsiders to understand to whom a book is dedicated, and even more why. In most cases, dedications are in no way random; there is some specific cause for them. In the case of the dedications in Stephen King's books I have taken a closer look at them, and want to share with you some of the more special among them, and the reasons for them.

Book: *Carrie* (Doubleday, 1974)
Dedication: *This is for Tabby, who got me into it – and then bailed me out of it.*
Explanation: Tabby is a nickname for Stephen King's wife Tabitha. *Carrie* was his first published book; King himself had written the beginning of it, found it wanting, and discarded it. Tabitha King picked it out of his wastebasket, convinced him to finish it, and after *Carrie* everything else followed.

Book: *The Shining* (Doubleday, 1977)
Dedication: *This is for Joe Hill King, who shines on.*
Explanation: Joe, the oldest son to Stephen and Tabitha King, was born in 1972 and according to those who know him personally has always had a kind of "shine", an openness. Possibly that is what is alluded to here. Or maybe King simply thought it fit in with the book's title (just as he did when he wrote "For Hans-Åke Lilja – keep shining on!" in my book *Shining in the Dark* [Cemetery Dance, 2017]).

Book: *Rage* (as by Richard Bachman, Signet, 1977)
Dedication: *For Susan Artz and WGT.*
Explanation: Susan Artz was one of King's earliest teachers. In manuscript, this novel was called *Getting It On*, and at that time it was dedicated to her alone. WGT stands for William G. Thompson, who was King's editor at Doubleday. Thompson several times tried to persuade Doubleday to publish *Getting It On*, but never succeeded. Finally, it was released as an original paperback and under the pen name ”Richard Bachman”. Though since King at the time kept his ”Bachman” pseudonym secret, it was perhaps a bit risky to dedicate the novel to two persons so close to him.

Book: *Pet Sematary* (Doubleday, 1983)
Dedication: *For Kirby McCauley.*
Explanation: Kirby McCauley (1941–2014) was Stephen King's first literary agent, helped him keep the ”Richard Bachman” pen name secret and took out the copyright on all except the first of the Bachman's novels in his own name, and was as well a personal friend of the Kings.

Book: *Thinner* (New American Library, 1984)
Dedication: *To my wife, Claudia Inez Bachman*
Explanation: In the made up story of ”Richard Bachman”, he was married to Claudia and had a son who was never named but who had according to the story fallen through the lid covering the well on the family farm and tragically drowned. Since *Thinner* was the first of the Bachman novels to be published in hardcover, it was for obvious reasons he dedicated it to his wife.

Book: *Misery* (Viking, 1987)
Dedication: *This is for Stephanie and Jim Leonard, who know why. Boy, do they.*
Explanation: Stephanie is Tabitha King's sister and was the editor of *Castle Rock*, a monthly newsletter for Stephen King enthusiasts and readers published from January, 1985, until December, 1989.

For a time she was also King's assistant. Jim, Stephanie's husband, took care of the King family's house. Both of them met quite a few King fans in their respective functions.

Book: *The Dark Half* (Viking, 1989)
Dedication: *This book is for Shirley Sonderegger, who helps me mind my business, and for her husband, Peter.*
Explanation: Shirley Sonderegger handled all of King's correspondence with readers during most of the 1980s. She has said that among the more bizarre parcels she opened was one containing the furs and skeletons of kittens, and another containing a scorpion. She is obviously married to Peter.

Book: *The Dark Tower III: The Waste Lands* (Donald M. Grant, 1991)
Dedication: *This third volume of the tale is gratefully dedicated to my son, OWEN PHILIP KING: Khef, ka, and Ka-tet.*
Explanation: Another dedication to King's youngest son Owen (to whom he had earlier dedicated *The Dead Zone*, 1979). At StephenKing.com there is a glossary explaining the made-up words in "The Dark Tower" series of books, and if you look under "High Speech" you find these explanations for the three words used in the dedication:
Khef = Literally speaking, *khef* means "the sharing of water." It also implies birth, life force, and all that is essential to existence. Khef can only be shared by those whom destiny has welded together for good or ill—in other words, by those who are Ka-tet.
Ka = It signifies life force, consciousness, duty, and destiny.
Ka-tet = *Ka-tet* means "one made from many." *Ka* refers to destiny; *tet* refers to a group of people with the same interests or goals. Ka-tet is the place where men's lives are joined by fate.
Book: *The Dark Tower VII: The Dark Tower* (Donald M. Grant/ Scribner 2004)

Dedication: *He who speaks without an attentive ear is mute. Therefore, Constant Reader, this final book in the Dark Tower cycle is dedicated to you. Long days and pleasant nights.*
Explanation: This is where Stephen King thanks all the readers who have followed the story of Roland and his friends and enemies, and where he points out that lacking his readers, his words would have had no audience and so found no listeners.

Book: *Never Flinch* (Scribner, 2025)
Dedication: *For Robin Furth, with love and thanks for all your hard work.*
Explanation: Robin Furth began working as a researcher for King when he began writing volumes five, six, and seven of The Dark Tower series. She later helped him also with research for other books and with other tasks.

An interview with Jim Bishop

In 2016 an extremely interesting but also unexpected book appeared: Hearts in Suspension (University of Maine Press), edited by Jim Bishop. It is basically an anthology of texts all centered on Stephen King's years as an undergraduate at the University of Maine, where Professor Bishop was one of his teachers, and King himself, along with a number of his fellow students, contribute essays.

Some interviews are hard to do; others very easy. Some people I talk to give very brief answers, sometimes even shorter than the question itself. Others talk on forever. Then we have Jim Bishop. He agreed to answer a few questions about the book *Hearts in Suspension* for me. I sent him about 10 questions and really didn't know what to expect … which is of course normal when you don't know the person you're interviewing. But boy, was I surprised. Not only did he give me excellent answers, he sent me (in his words) a two page "short narrative" that was so much better than any back-and-fort interview of questions and answers. So thanks, Jim, it was a pleasure to "interview" you…even if you did most of the work yourself.

The interview:

By way of introduction, I retired a few years ago as a lecturer in the English department of the University of Maine, where, decades earlier, I had Steve as a student in what was his first class (Freshman Comp) there. I also co-taught a memorable seminar in contemporary poetry with Burt Hatlen in which Steve and some of the essayists in "Hearts in Suspension," as well as Tabitha Spruce (now King), were very active participants. Some of them comment on that seminar in the book.

You ask about the genesis of "Hearts in Suspension." You know, ideas happen – who knows where they come from. I had always thought that "Hearts in Atlantis" (the novella), for all its bad-boy vibe (even the names: Ronnie Malenfant), really plumbed a much deeper and more heartfelt current. I thought Steve really caught something in that story of what it felt like to be a working class kid, coming of age in the boil of the late '60s, with all the highs and heartaches of that formative time of life, with the added charge of the student movements, the sense of hope and promise in all that, but looming over it all, the toxic shadow of the Vietnam war and the draft. And at the edge of it all, the encroaching awareness on the part of Peter Riley, Steve's avatar in the narrative, that he was approaching that one-way door to adulthood, whatever robberies that might entail. In late summer of 2015, as we were approaching the 50th anniversary year of Steve' entrance as a student into UMaine in the fall of 2016, it occurred to me that it would be interesting if Steve were to write an essay – a nonfiction narrative – looking back at his student days, and to pair his nonfiction take with the fictionalized version. So, in August, 2015, I proposed it to him. "Pitched" it, as he said. I could see Steve was understandably reluctant at first to reenter those murky waters, but thankfully he decided to take the plunge (and, by the way, to donate what would have been his proceeds from the book to the University of Maine Press). I also suggested that we ask some of Steve's fellow students from the time to write accompanying essays, recounting their own experience of those formative years. Steve loved that idea. And so I set about tracking them down, one by one. And we were on our way.

I can't know what might have gone through the minds of the several former students when I first contacted them with my proposal, but just try to imagine, if you even can, what it would be like for them to be asked, out of the proverbial blue, to dredge back into their own memories of those lost Atlantis years, half a century distant. A time when most of the readers of this book, I imagine, would not have been even a devilish twinkle in their parents' eyes. And they were given no restrictions or topic guidelines, by Stephen or myself, except to try to recapture what they could of their own memories of that time and to assemble them into some kind of coherent narrative. Pretty damn gutsy on their part, these refugees from that sunken Atlantis of the '60s – that they took on the challenge and plunged in. I tried to edit as lightly as possible in the process, to maintain their individual voices and manners of expression. I read their drafts and made my suggestions, but told them that they would be the final arbiters of their essays. Kudos to them for taking it on and for what has come together as a result.

I also want to give a special commendation here to Steve, not only for agreeing to give my original proposal a try, but for approaching this operation (in every sense) with candor and an open heart. It sure wasn't a walk in the park, plunging back there into that fraught time – he took it on, and I think his readers will agree that the result was something special. I want to mention as well that, as editor of this collection, one of my principal responsibilities was to respond to Stephen's early drafts with my editorial suggestions. Well, I'd edited his writing 50 years ago, in freshman comp, but he'd been down a few narrative roads since then, and I wondered how he'd react to his old prof, the ghost of Christmas Past, again blue-penciling his compositions. I have to say, he was absolutely a pro in all his dealings with me – accepted a number of my suggestions, which he thought appropriate, and stood pat on others. Nothing high-handed or divaish in any part of the exchange. And an amusing sidelight: I later submitted my own essay to him for his examination, even though he hadn't asked to review it. He sent me a very few suggestions, which were indeed helpful. But he also added that editing his old prof had a decidedly Freudian dimension. Well, son, we both survived it.

You ask, Lilja, about the aftermath of the book's publication – what reactions I've received from readers. It's still very early, less than two weeks after the book's release as I write this, but everything I've heard so far has been very positive. I just read in a local newspaper, for example, that "Hearts…" was one reader's favorite book in the last year. Another reader wrote to the UMaine Press that she cried reading the book, having to do, I think, with the spirit of hope and belief in the possibilities of collective effort that the book chronicles. I'm personally struck by the sheer coincidence that the book was released the day before our Presidential election in the U.S. Or are there really coincidences? Call it a striking synchronicity. Strangely, the spirit that comes through this collection of voices has become for me personally a kind of smelling salts and reviver of my own spirit in the wake of that election.

As for my own new-found visibility in the wake of the book's emergence, well, yes, I've been asked for an autograph or two – ha ha. Clearly, at the age of 77, this is my five minutes in the sun, right? OK, so allow me to bask a minute in this celebrity-by-association. This too shall pass. What is far more meaningful is the book itself, now finding its way into the world, with no further need of mothering or fathering from this corner. I wish it well and hope it finds its way into the hands of your readers. I would welcome any feedback through your site.

From Molly to Chinga to Bunghoney

Writing scripts for an ongoing TV series can hardly be simple, not even if you are a professional. Stephen King learned this when he wrote a script for *The X-Files*, which ran on Fox for nine seasons from 1993 until 2002. King's episode was finally aired as episode 10 of season five and originally aired on February 8, 1998. It was entitled ”Chinga”, but King's manuscript was titled ”Molly”, the name of the doll that causes all the problems. Chris Carter, the show's creator and executive producer, change the title to ”Chinga”, either because he was unaware of, or just didn't care, that ”chinga” is Spanish means ”fuck you”. Which is why the episode when shown outside of the US was called ”Bunghoney”.

Many *X-Files* fans however felt that the episode didn't feel quite like a genuine part of the series. The plot didn't hold together, the writing seemed strange and a bit clumsy. Most of the guilt for this probably belonged to Chris Carter himself, who had rewritten the script so many times that practically nothing by King himself was left in the final version.

Carter argued that his changes were justified because King simply wasn't used to write for the show:

”Stephen wasn't used to writing for Mulder and Scully… the Mulder-and-Scully story in his original draft didn't quite work.”

In the episode Scully goes to Maine and ends up in the middle of a case centered on a series of murders committed in a grocery store. While helping the local police solve the case, she begins suspecting that a doll belonging to a young girl is the culprit. She reaches this conclusion basically without any assistance from Mulder, whose comments and suggestions she gets only in brief telephone conversations. This idea was King's, but initially he let Scully be a victim in the grocery store massacre and let Mulder turn up in a vision, guiding her along in solving the case. In Carter's opinion, this was too weird even for *X Files,* and by not letting Scully solve the case without Mulder's help also portrayed her as incompetent.

If you read King's manuscript, you quickly find a number of things not retained in the filmed episode. Instead of people hurting themselves when the see Molly reflected, Molly's mother has premonitions in the form of mirror images of who will die. In the episode, it is the doll Molly itself that is an evil force; you might guess that it is in some way possessed, but this is never confirmed. In King's manuscript, it is clear that some kind of being is inside the doll, and at the end the being is even forced to leave the doll, then disappears from having nowhere to go. Additionally, Carter chose to make Polly, the girl owning Molly, into less of an introvert. In the episode, it is Polly who screams and threatens along with Molly's "I want to play", while in King's version Polly was almost catatonic, mostly just staring.

Anyone who hasn't read the manuscript will probably not view these changes as problematic. You can't miss what you've never known. And while I'm no *X Files* expert, Carter's claim that King was unable to give a consistent portrayal of Mulder and Scully seems far-fetched to me. The difference in their portrayals between the manuscript and the episode is only marginal.

When Stephen King wrote his script, no romance between Mulder and Scully had as yet appeared in the serial, and it wouldn't do so for quite a while yet. But King had the notion that sooner or later such feelings would develop, so in his manuscript Scully says things to Mulder like, "I love it when you talk dirty", and, "I guess I just miss the sound of your voice", and when the two reunite at the end of King's version, he describes it as "a classic lovers' shot, profiles like you'd see on a Valentine's heart." But in the end, Carter deleted all the flirting in King's script before filming the segment.

The segment director, Kim Manners, has confirmed that "The nuts and bolts were [King's], but ["Chinga"] was really one of Chris' scripts." And that script wasn't so much by King as a nod to King's stories. It is set in Maine, and we often hear characters say ”ayuh”, as they frequently do in King's stories. Additionally, though King had not published his short story ”1408” at the time, perhaps we get a premonition of it when in one scene we can read a text saying, ”Melissa Turner's home 14:08”. Or perhaps I'm just making too much of a chance occurrence of that particular number … which actually seems most likely.

Interlude 4: Props/Promotion

A central part of film making is ”props”, which means all the specific things used by the actors or just present in the images we see. As viewers, we obviously feel that those things simply make up the background to whatever is happening, but that is far from the whole story. Everything that will be visible is carefully thought out and has a purpose. In the following interview with Jim Murray he explains what a ”props master”, which is the correct title for him and his colleagues, actually does. His stories are, I think, extremely interesting.

Personally I have a small collection of things which have appeared in films made from Stephen King's stories. It includes John F. Kennedy campaign buttons from the TV series *11.22.62* (2016), given me by Jim Murray. There are also a copy of a newspaper and a supplement, both of *The Castle Rock Times*, on view in the shopping center in *The Mist* (2007), which were donated to my collection by Frank Darabont. I call my collection ”Marv's Museum”, Marv being the cartoon figure featured in the Lilja's Library logo.

Apart from those things there is also a book, purported to be written by the author Mike Noonan, who is a character in *Bag of Bones* (2011). In the film, Noonan is played by Pierce Brosnan, who has signed this particular copy with his character 's name. The book was also used in a promotion campaign where a signing event at Lilja's Library was announced.

If you'd like to take a look at these and the other objects in my online museum, you can do so at liljas-library.com.

—MARV'S MUSEUM—

A division of Lilja's Library

In this museum you will find Stephen King related props and other interesting items. Click on the thumbnails to open the galleries...

The Dark Tower Pilot

Gerald's Game

Christine

11.22.63 Director's Chair

JFK Campaign Pins

Paranoid

Haven season 1, ep. 8: Ain't No Sunshine

Haven season 2, ep. 1: A Tale of Two Audreys

Bag of Bones

Dolan's Cadillac

The Mist

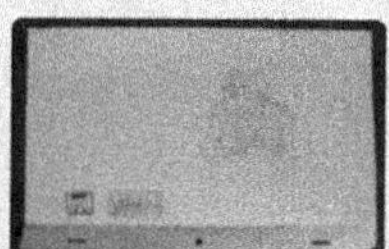
Home Delivery

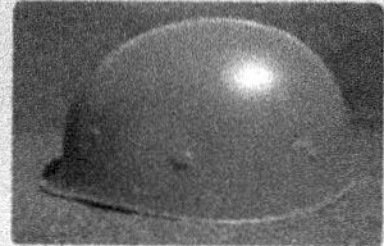
Battleground

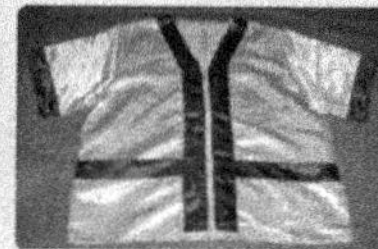
The Dead Zone (The Combination)

Desperation

An interview with Jim Murray

This interview was conducted on April 9, 2016, not long after the *11.22.63* miniseries had aired on Hulu. Jim had worked on the serial as property master – usually shortened to props master – and was kind enough to make time for talking to me about the series and his role in creating it.

Jim Murray: My official title is props master or property master depending on which show. So I basically take care of anything that the actors touch. So a good example of that would be, let's use *11.22.63* for example. The Yellow Card Man had the yellow card so I have to figure out what the yellow card was and either build, find or get it. Or the sledgehammer that was used, the different weapons, any food, all recording equipment. Anything that the actors interact with is what I take care of. Stuff like desks, table lamps, chairs, carpets that is all taken care of with the set deck department. Obviously an actor sits on a chair, that's not me, but if there is a bomb attached to the chair that would be me. Or if the actor turns over and grabs a pen and starts writing on a piece of paper, the pen and paper would be me. And I have to work to make sure that everything works with everyone's look. So there is a certain look we pick and then we have to make sure we stay under that umbrella for that look.

Lilja: How long in advance do you start planning for a film or TV series? There is a lot of stuff you need to find or make.

Jim Murray: Well, just think about your everyday life. You got your bag, you go to work and everything you have in your bag is stuff you have as a person. So when you're on a show you have to start thinking of those characters and what they use. For instance

Jake, he's got all of this stuff and he is a character and James Franco is going to want to play him in a certain way and we see him in a couple of different time periods. So anything that he would have will help establish him as a character, as the things you have would in your life. You got your car key, you got your water bottle, you got your satchel and you got everything in your satchel. You got your wallet and in it you might have photos of your kids or some money or receipts. I flesh all of those things out. And depending on who the actor is and how detailed they want to get, some of those actors got stuff that we don't even see, we create character things. Some might want to have things in their pocket because they are establishing the character. We don't see those props but they are there to help that actor get into the role. So depending on the project it dictates how much time I get. For *11.22.63* I think I had six to eight weeks. Maybe eight weeks to prep.

And movies are like circuses. We move into town, set up, do what we need to do, we tear down and go away. So I would go in and break down the scripts, figure out what all the stuff is, have a meeting with the director and the designer because I'm usually hired by the designer. Some request me because they have worked with me before and they like me. Some like me because I can stay on budget. Once I have all my meetings I put together a budget and sometimes they say we have like 100,000 dollars for props or you have this much and I'll have to tell them what they can get for that. If they want more they have to increase the budget.

Because *11.22.63* was a period show it was much easier to work on in the sense that we have historical references on everything from the beginning to end. We know what the JFK campaign buttons looked like. We know things from that time so working on a period piece is much easier than say a space show that's set 20 years in the future. We can do what we want but that is harder than doing historical pieces. There are a lot of rental houses where we rent our stuff and if we know that we're doing a 60's thing I just send out the buyers to the antique shops to get stuff from that period for the background stuff. Anything character or script specific we'll look for on eBay or Amazon or build it if we can't find it.

Lilja: When did you start working with props?

Jim Murray: I first started doing props like 25 years ago and it was a lot harder because there was no internet. We used phone books and you were limited to what you could do but now I do probably 60-70% of my prop shopping online and have the stuff sent to me because I can shop the world now and get better options. So if it requires an antique sledgehammer from 1960 I could just type that on eBay and cross-reference it with historical photos and buy it rather than to go to 30 or 40 stores.

Lilja: What happens with everything you buy for a show? Do you store it?

Jim Murray: They tend to want to rent as much as possible because then there is no stuff for them to deal with at the end of the shooting. With *11.22.63* being a miniseries we knew we weren't going back so what basically happened was that we purchased a lot, rented a lot and they, at the end of it, put it in a trailer and sold it at a set sale.

Lilja: So then you have to do it all over if you do another movie about the JFK assassination?

Jim Murray: Yeah. All of our stuff from *11.22.63* is gone and there is a new miniseries, a sequel to *The Kennedys* and none of our stuff is available to them. It's frustrating.

Lilja: But there is a market for people to rent out stuff to movies?

Jim Murray: Yes, I got all kind of different vendors that rent me stuff. There is pretty much vendors for everything.

Lilja: So you can actually make a movie and then go to a movie years later and find stuff that you used in your movie?

Jim Murray: Yes. If I know that certain things have been rented a lot I try to avoid them. And we make a lot of stuff ourself. All the files in *11.22.63*, Al's files, those were scratch built. We built them from scratch. I sent them out to someone who does all my paper stuff. All their focus is on building me paper stuff. So that photo that Bill has of his sister, we took that photo, the art department put it on paper and I sent it out to my paper builder to age and to cut the corner and all that stuff on it.

Lilja: And I guess you make multiples of everything if something should happen to break?

Jim Murray: Yeah, once we start rolling on a TV series or a movie it's no stopping it. You don't want to be the department that slows it down because if you do you have a problem. You probably won't get hired again. And everything breaks. Cause if you give an actor a glass and they drop it in a reset you need to go "wait I got another one". So we avoid buying a 3000 dollar crystal glass because they might break. We always have doubles to the hero of everything. The hero meaning the one we see the most of. So if the actors wear a watch we always buy a second watch so if we lose the watch we have another. So we have to budget for that and that is why a pen in my breakdown costs 50-100 bucks. It might only be a three or ten dollar pen but I have to buy six pens. Show the six pens to the director, decide which one we want to use. Return the others and then buy more of the one we picked. So nothing is like just getting one.

Lilja: Are you trusted to handle all that or do you have to run it by the director?

Jim Murray: It depends on the director. Some trust me and know my judgement but it's always best to show everything to everyone.

What you don't want is someone on set, we might be shooting at two o'clock in the morning in a rural area and the director goes "What the **** is this? I hate this!" You don't want that to happen.

Lilja: What was the biggest challenge with *11.22.63*?

Jim Murray: The biggest challenge for *11.22.63* was when you work with a book you already have a fan base. So what you have are people that have already planned it and mapped it and seen it in their minds because they read the source material. So the hardest thing is to be true to what the director wants while being true to what the fans expect from having read it already. It's much easier if it's something new that no one has read already. We try our best but we are always going to disappoint people and that's probably the hardest thing.

Lilja: Do you read the book as well or do you just focus on the script?

Jim Murray: I tend to read the books. I think it's important to understand the source material. Sometimes it's good and sometimes it's bad because sometimes the scripts we get are very different from the book. I think it's also good to read the book because what you can do is you can tip the hat to the people who read it and put in subtle things that others miss, because I deal in the world of things that people touch. So the book might have specific things like the yellow card, things that people connect with when they read the book. If there is a name in the book that we can reference to on somebody's name tag the hardcore fans see those things. I think that is important.

Lilja: And it's interesting. If you do a good job people won't notice your job.

Jim Murray: Exactly. If we get it right you don't notice. If we get it wrong you notice. I have been on shows that takes place in the

40's and they didn't have the budget to get it right. I brought that up but they didn't care. They said no one would notice but people do notice. The easiest show to work on is a contemporary show because I can just run out and buy things. It exists. Everything in the future has to be built because it doesn't exists and anything not contemporary has to be historically right. We try to get it right but sometimes the ball is dropped or there isn't budget for it and we don't get it right.

Lilja: Yeah, and then we can read about it on IMDB.

Jim Murray: Exactly! And it always happens.

Lilja: Yeah and I think that as a viewer it's kind of fun to find those small things but I guess you don't think so since it's your job? [laughs]

Jim Murray: Absolutely, it's totally entertainment when it's not my show [laughs]. And it bothers me when there is a wrong way to do it and a right way to do it and they pick the wrong one. It's on me as the props master. It's not like I can put a disclaimer saying, "Jim Murray didn't pick this prop, somebody else did that". It reflects badly on my work. But then I am a contractor and what you want is what I'm going to get you because that is my job.

Lilja: How much of an expert are you on stuff after having researched so much for shows and films?

Jim Murray: I have done movies in 1864 in New York, space shows, drugs shows and a lot more shows and I become an expert for the time I need to be an expert and then I generally forget about a lot of things. Right now I know a lot about the 60's and I know a lot about the Kennedys, but a lot of the stuff I won't hold on to.

Lilja: When you go in stores as a private person, do you constantly see stuff that you can use in upcoming movies?

Jim Murray: Yeah, I'm constantly stockpiling ideas in my head that I could use later on. You do look at the world differently when you're a prop master. Always looking for interesting things. And if you said to me "Jim, I need to find this…" I could probably find it for you. I'm really good at sourcing stuff.

Lilja: Have you done any other Stephen King stuff?

Jim Murray: No, I haven't and the one day he was on set I missed him…

Lilja: Hopefully you'll get a chance to work on another King adaptation. Thank you so much for taking the time to speak to me. I enjoyed this behind the scenes tour a lot.

Inside View: Stephen King's own gossip magazine

That Stephen King is fascinated by stories that tend to stretch the truth will hardly surprise anyone. In fact, he has made it clear in a posting on Twitter:

"Hey, do you guys remember that supermarket tabloid that used to have stories about BatBoy? Man, I loved that shit."

Most probably he is thinking of magazines like *The National Enquirer* and similar publications. And the fact is that he likes them to the extent of having created his own version of them, *Inside View*. But it exists only in King's imagination and in a number of his stories.

The first time we hear of this magazine is in *The Dead Zone* (Viking, 1979). Richard Dees, a journalist at *Inside View*, gets in touch with the novel's protagonist, Johnny Smith, and makes him an offer. He wants Johnny to write a column where he shows off his "powers". Johnny politely but firmly rejects this offer and throws Dees out of his home.

But Richard Dees isn't that easily banished. In the novelette "The Night Fler" (included in *Nightmares and Dreamscapes*) both *Inside View* and Richard Dees pop up again. Dees is now a more experienced and also cynical man than when we met him in *The Dead Zone*; we are told that he now holds to a motto that tells him to "Never print anything he believes and never believe anything he prints."

Inside View has turned up again in more of Stephen King's stories, but plays an important part in the plot only in *The Dead Zone* and "The Night Flier". Otherwise, it is just one of the recurring staples of King's fictional world that he sometimes mentions in his stories, just as the towns he has invented are mentioned along with others we know from our own world. Here are a few examples of how *Inside View* occurs in other stories.

- In "Popsy", Briggs Sheridan refers to advertisements in *Inside View* and *The National Enquirer*.

- In "Home Delivery", *Inside View* is mentioned as having been the first American paper to report on the zombie outbreak in Thumper, Florida.

- In *Bag of Bones*, Mike Noonan speculates on whether *Inside View* might be interested in writing about a custody case.

- In "Big Driver", Tessa Jean wonders if her case might risk ending up in *Inside View* if she reports it to the police.

- In *Joyland*, according to Devin Jones the occurrences at the end of the novel were written up in a number of news outlets, among them *Inside View*.

- In *Doctor Sleep*, Lucy Stone mentions that she doesn't want her daughter Abra's name appearing in *Inside View*.

- In *End of Watch*, *Inside View* is one of the newspapers and magazines found in Martine Stover's and Janice Ellerton's home.

- In *Elevation*, Scott Carey says that he has no intention of ending up in *Inside View*, squeezed in between The Night Flier and Slender Man.

- In ”If It Bleeds”, Holly Gibney threatens the outsider (at the time disguised as Chet Ondowsky) with reporting his activities to *Inside View*. She also mentions that the magazine has already spent a year writing about The Night Flier and two writing about Slender Man.

- In *Billy Summers*, Billy reflects that his two partners Nick Majarian and Giorgio Piglitelli probably believes him (in his guise as dumb Billy) to be someone who would read *Star Magazine*, *Archie* comics and *Inside View*.

- In *Fairy Tale*, Charlie Reade expresses his skepticism about royalty in his world, calling them ”fodder for supermarket tabloids like the *National Enquirer* and *Inside View*.”

- In *Holly*, Holly Gibney is surprised that an article published in *Bell College of Arts and Sciences* has the same ”nudge-nudge, wink-wink” tone as those published in *Inside View*. And after the murders committed by Rodney and Emily Harris have been revealed, Jerome Robinsons says to Izzy Jaynes that the families of the victims must be informed before the details appear in *Inside View*.

- Finally, in ”Rattlesnakes” (in *You Like It Darker*), Becky views Inside View her favorite paper and learns from it that Queen Elizabeth’s ghost haunts Balmoral Castle and that there is a civilization of intelligent ants hidden deep in the Amazon rainforest.

It remains to be seen if *Inside View* makes further appearances. Personally I wouldn’t be surprised, and if I ever get the chance, I will definitely get a subscription to it.

An interview with Steve Coulson of Campfire

When the A&E (stands for Arts & Entertainment) TV network wanted to promote its *Bag of Bones* miniseries, the company chosen to produce a successful campaign was Campfire in New York. I wanted to know how they did it, and for that reason on December 5, 2011, interviewed Steve Coulson, who is Creative Director at Campfire.

Lilja: Please tell me about Campfire, the company that created the site DarkScoreStories.com.

Steve Coulson: Campfire is a marketing company in New York City that works with a variety of clients and brands, to connect them with fans and audiences using storytelling techniques. Two of our founders were part of the group that made *The Blair Witch Project*, and some of the lessons learnt then about engaging and exciting fans to drive brand success permeates all our work.

Lilja: Tell me about Dark Score Stories. How did it happen and who came up with the idea?

Steve Coulson: It's sometimes hard to pin down the exact moment that an idea comes into being, especially when you're creating something with multiple layers for multiple audiences like Dark Score Stories. Some of the elements evolved slowly during our initial ideation process.

But there were definitely two things that provided a springboard. One was the A&E Marketing team who very early on said that it would be interesting to explore the history of Dark Score Lake through interviews with its residents. And that idea is the underpinning of everything.

The other was Matt Venne's script for *Bag of Bones*, which we read before shooting. And without giving away any secrets (and to be honest I can't be sure if the final cut is the same as the script), Matt's original draft had several specific references to the Stephen King universe that only dedicated fans would notice, as "Easter Eggs". And that got us thinking that an interactive experience could dive even deeper into that territory.

Lilja: What was your part in all this?

Steve Coulson: My job as Creative Director of the transmedia tune-in piece is to make sure we're staying completely true to both Mick Garris' and Stephen King's vision of Dark Score Lake, while telling a story that's unique to the mediums we use. It has to intrigue very casual fans and induce them to watch the show without being too complex, yet satisfy the legion of Stephen King fans who actively want it to be layered and explorable. Luckily, I am a HUGE Stephen King fan myself (as you can probably tell from the site), so in many ways this was my dream assignment. We felt a lot of pressure to do Mr. King's work and fans justice, and the reaction on sites like yours has been very gratifying.

Lilja: The site if full of Stephen King references, how did you came up with all of them?

Steve Coulson: We worked alongside one of our favorite collaborators, the author J.C. Hutchins, who, too is a big King fan (he's the one wearing the Dr. Love T shirt in the bookstore). Between us we scoured the novels and short stories and made lists of hundreds of potential items to include. Our aim was to make sure each work was referenced at least once, and I think we did that (at least, every book, if not every short story)

We also relied on a few King Encyclopedias and, of course, lots of googling :)

Lilja: It must have taken forever to get all those references right? How many people were involved in creating these photos?

Steve Coulson: It was actually a three step process. First we defined all the unusual objects that we thought we needed to buy and put on set, and then scoured junk shops and online stores to get them over a 2-3 week period.

The second step was to create printed material that we felt we needed to have on set to place in the scene. That would include things like all the covers for the books that were wrapped and placed in the book store, the posters on the wall of the music store.

Finally after the shoot, a lot of things were retouched into the scenes. I would say perhaps 40-50% of the things you see never actually existed physically, like the record covers and a lot of the props in the junk store.

It's a very small team that worked very long hours :-)

Lilja: Tell me a bit about the photo shoots themselves.

Steve Coulson: After a lot of searching and looking at portfolios, we were lucky enough to secure Joachim Ladefoged, an amazing photojournalist from Europe, who flew over to join our team on set in Nova Scotia for the shoot. The animated gifs are created by shooting High Definition video which is then manipulated in post-production, so the key images were very controlled. But after that, Joachim was able to take a more photojournalistic approach and shoot scenes as they were improvised by actors. We took thousands of photographs across the seven stories, and then selected the best 70 or so for the site.

The other thing we did was work with the actors to record the audio tracks on set. We had working scripts but then all the actors improvised around the scene and gave us some wonderful material.

Lilja: Some of the people there I recognize but not all. Are they from the series or handpicked for the photos?

Steve Coulson: Obviously we wanted to feature as many of the cast as we could, but that still left some holes in our story. Clearly we couldn't feature Sara Tidwell directly, so we invented the character of the Music Store owner to tell a little more of her backstory.

And the Junk Store owner is another invention purely for the site. He serves the dual purpose of allowing us to include a LOT of Stephen King Universe artifacts in his store, while at the same time hinting of the community's dark past - Dark Score Lake is a place where a lot of children's toys seem to wind up unplayed with. And fans of other Stephen King novels and short stories might find something vaguely recognizable in Gerald Lean.

Lilja: There is also a book with all the photos in it. Will this one be sold in stores or how can fans get it? Is it very limited?

Steve Coulson: The book was printed in a very limited quantity, and mostly shipped out to journalists and bloggers. There were a few left over for fan sites to give away as prizes, but apart from that, they're unavailable anywhere. So if you get your hands on one, it's a collector's item :)

Lilja: Is there anything else hidden away on the site?

Steve Coulson: Oh yes, I don't think anyone has found everything yet. There are seven hidden video sequences and Get Glue badges, and at least three ghosts haunt the photos - if you can find them :)

Lilja: Anything else you'd like to add?

Steve Coulson: We're really glad that fans loved the prequel story of Dark Score Lake, but remember, that's just the appetizer. The main course, as served up by Master Chef Mick Garris, comes to the table on December 11th, so make sure you tune in for *Bag of Bones*. It's going to be amazing.

Lilja: I'm sure everyone will be watching. Thanks for talking to me.

The long and winding road to The Dark Tower

Stephen King's series "The Dark Tower" have been called many things. King's magnum opus. King's masterpiece. Many readers (like me) have lived for a long time with this work. Its first volume consists of five short stories, all of them originally published in *The Magazine of Fantasy and Science Fiction*, the first of them in the October, 1978. The last and seventh book in the series was published on Stephen King's 57th birthday, September 21, 2004. After that, King went back to Roland Deschain and his companions in *The Wind Through the Keyhole* in 2012. In addition to this, since 2007 a large number of comic books have appeared, based both on the published books and on original material (written by Robin Furth, King's long-time personal research assistant, and Peter David). But here my intent is to focus instead on the various attempts to film the story, attempts which so far have winded on for almost two decades, led to one disappointing result and leads on into the future.

The first time an attempt to film the books was heard of on February 13, 2007, when it was reported that producer, director and script writer J. J. Abrams intended to film the books, although it remained uncertain whether he would do it as a feature film or a TV series. Regardless of that, everyone reacted positively. At last Roland would come to the silver screen (or possibly the TV screen, but still). Then nothing happened.

In March, it turned out that in fact nothing much had ever happened. A clarification of the situation was posted on Stephen King's message board:

"I asked Steve for clarification on this and his response was that no deal has been finalized. If and when one is, it will be a 3 year option which he will sell them for $19."

Those who have read the books will know that the number "19" plays a considerable role in the series, and why King picked that particular amount.

This led to Abrams also been asked for comments, and in an interview with Wired News he said:

"This is something that we are just now talking about with Stephen, so it's too early for me to say that we're even officially doing it yet just because the thing is in the early stages of discussion. I love what the *The Dark Tower* is. Damon Lindelof is obsessed (with it)."

Obviously, then, any actual film was far from as close in time as many had hoped; plans were only at a very tentative early stage.

The next statement was made by producer and script writer Damon Lindelof in September, 2008, and gave no positive news:

"*The Dark Tower* is to me every bit as daunting an adaptation as the *Lord of the Rings* trilogy must have been for Peter Jackson, except we've got seven books we're looking at. There are always *Dark Tower* conversations, but the figuring out of what this will look like as a movie has not begun."

Basically, then, nothing at all had happened in the next year and a half. A year later, it became obvious that Abrams and Lindelof would not film the books; on November 11, 2009, Abrams stated to MTV News:

"*The Dark Tower* thing is tricky. It's such an important piece of writing. The truth is that Damon and I are not looking at that right now."

Less than half a year later, it was again time to start hoping. On April 30, 2010, it was announced that "The Dark Tower" series was to be made into three feature films which would be completed by a TV series. Akiva Goldman would write the script, Ron Howard direct and Brian Grazer produce. This sounded almost too good to be true. On May 1, Stephen King published a comment:

"It looks good. Things are happening and they are happening fast but any reports you see might be taken with a grain of salt for the next couple of weeks. You will know the news from the official source as soon as we are able to post it."

Four months later, September 9, a press release was published on King's Internet site stating that the plan was to produce a feature film, then a TV series, another feature, another TV series, and a final feature film. Many, and I include myself among them, were exalted at this. Would we really be treated to this generous opulence? Already on September 10, King gave further thoughts in an interview published by *Entertainment Weekly*:

"I always thought it would take more than a single movie, but I didn't see this solution coming — i.e., several movies and TV series. It was Ron [Howard] and Akiva [Goldsman]'s idea. Once it was raised, I thought at once it was the solution."

Did he have any ideal actors to play Roland, Eddie, Susannah, or Jake?

"The *Twilight* cast, of course! Just kidding. I haven't got as far as casting in my thoughts, but when I write about Susannah Dean, I always kind of see Angela Bassett in my mind's eye. Mostly I just want good people in those parts. Ron Howard will find them, I'm sure."

He was, however, very clear on what role he himself wanted to play: "I'd love to be the voice of Blaine the Mono."

In October, 2010, NBC (which was set to air the TV series) published its listing of next season's serials, where the following text was included:

DARK TOWER, THE: Eerie, dreamlike, set in a world that is weirdly related to our own, The Gunslinger introduces Roland Deschain of Gilead, of In-World that was, as he pursues his enigmatic antagonist to the mountains that separate the desert from the Western Sea. Roland is a solitary figure, perhaps accursed, who with a strange singlemindedness traverses an exhausted, almost timeless landscape. The people he encounters are left behind, or worse – left dead. At a way station, however, he meets Jake, a boy from a particular time (1977) and a particular place (New York City), and soon the two are joined – khef, ka, and ka-tet. The mountains lie before them. So does the man in black and, somewhere far beyond ... the Dark Tower.

The first feature film was scheduled for May 17, 2013. So we would be able to see the first season of the series in 2011 and the first feature in 2013. Then Ron Howard gave us an early Christmas present when on December 14, 2010, he offered this update on the project:

"It is going well, and it has been incredibly stimulating to work on. It's dense, a great author's life work is not to be taken lightly. It has been utterly fascinating to explore it, and we are having great creative conversations. I've begun tossing and turning at 3 in the morning over it, so that's a good sign."

The year 2011 began with speculations on who would be picked to play Roland. Several sources reported that either Javier Bardem or Viggo Mortensen would be chosen. But in an interview on January 20, Ron Howard stated that the final okay on the first feature film had not yet been given. This, however, was nothing to make much of; everything seemed to be moving along:

"I'm working on it. We don't know if it's a 'go' but it is picking up a lot of momentum and a lot of creative momentum."

In another interview, he talked about the extent of his involvement and also confirmed that the same actors would feature in both the film and the series.

"Right now what we're talking about is a movie and six or eight hours of television to bridge. My plan is to do most of those TV hours, if not all, and certainly the movies."

In spite of all these optimistic statements, I was not alone in worrying about Howard's comment that they had so far not had a final okay. Obviously we were many enough to make those handling Stephen King's official website publish this announcement on January 25, 2011:

"Steve just had a meeting with Ron Howard and Akiva Goldsman a couple weeks ago and the contracts have all been signed. I think he would have mentioned if there was a problem but he said the meeting went fine. My understanding is they're planning to start announcing casting choices, possibly this week."

Two days later, January 27, both Stephen King's website and other sources reported that Javier Bardem had been cast to play Roland:

"I have the official go-ahead to announce that Ron Howard/ Universal has offered Javier Bardem the part of Roland. I do not know if he has accepted the offer but chances are they wouldn't make this announcement if he wasn't considering it. The announcement was made through Deadline Hollywood."

And on April 26, this was officially confirmed:

Javier Bardem has officially signed an epic deal to star in the movie and TV adaptations of Stephen King's "Dark Tower" book series. The Oscar-winning actor will play Roland Deschain. Bardem has signed on to the first movie and the miniseries, but the intention is that he will star in all three movies and each of the TV series..

But no joy lasts forever. Already on May 6, only ten days later, it seems that someone must have started wondering about the cost of the project, and realizing that financing might prove to throw perhaps quite a few spanners in the works. *Variety* had spoken to an unnamed source at Universal and published a worrisome report:

Universal's unprecedented "Dark Tower" movie trilogy and interlocking TV series, seen as a hugely ambitious project from the start, may wind up being too big for the studio's appetite. Sources tell Variety that the project has run into budgetary complications that have caused Universal execs to rethink their original plans.

Hollywood Reporter ran with this and tree days later published a story on the project. Two sentences told the entire story: the entire project was once again touch and go:

"A final decision is said to be expected soon on whether to move forward, seek additional financing partners, or cancel the project entirely. But cast and crew have been told to stop prepping the project."

From there, everything went downhill. Reports grew steadily more negative and already by March 15, 2011, you could feel that this project would never materialize, or at the very least not in the form and with the resources initially hoped for:

"According to the *Hollywood Reporter*, Universal has dropped plans to start shooting this fall, as Goldsman is rewriting the script to reflect a lower budget,"

"After reports about *The Dark Tower* going into turn around at Universal, suddenly rumors abound that the epic Stephen King adaptation is now slated for a Ron Howard-directed February 2012 start date."

Ron Howard tried to keep a brave and positive face on, saying in an Entertainment Weekly interview that:

"We had to pull back to our September start date due to budget delays and ongoing story development and logistical issues, but Dark Tower is moving forward."

My suspicion is that most of those keeping their fingers crossed for the project to materialize had already given up hope, and on July 19 (always that number "19") it was confirmed. Universal officially stated that the company no longer had any plans for bringing "The Dark Tower" series to the screen. Howard and his team now either had to convince some other production company of taking over their project, or let it go. Stephen King also issued a comment:

"We had to pull back to our September start date due to budget delays and ongoing story development and logistical issues, but Dark Tower is moving forward."

During the remainder of 2011, statements from those involved kept appearing and every time claimed that the project was still alive and would be realized. You can wonder if anyone actually believed this, or if it was all a game of make believe in the hope of in spite of everything finding someone willing to finance the undertaking. HBO was mentioned as a partner on the TV series segment of the project. Warner was said to be involved. Bardem disappeared to play other parts; Russel Crowe was claimed to be the new actor to be cast as Roland. In August, 2012, Warner as well decided to take no part. Howard still stubbornly claimed that he had not given up, but things now looked darker than ever. In 2013, Netflix was claimed to be a possible partner, but that also came to nothing and instead rumors began circulating about it all being compressed into a single feature film. Seven books in a single movie? The idea seems to have been that if only the first feature did well, more would follow. But was it really possible to film the first book in a way that made audiences who were not part of the most devoted Stephen King readers like it well enough to make further films economically feasible? Though at least one positive development occurred when in January 2014 it was confirmed that Aaron Paul hade accepted to play Eddie Dean.

On June 19 (”19” again!), 2014, Stephen King issued a comment:

“I was very excited when Ron Howard got involved with that project. His original take on it was the best. He wanted to do the movies — three tentpole movies — interspersed with a number of TV series that covered Roland and his adventures as a young man. It was a brilliant concept, and I’m pretty sure it would have worked. [But] what sometimes happens in Hollywood and in filmmaking is, the financing fell apart, or the studio started to have second thoughts.”

But he still refused to abandon all hope:

“Sooner or later, it’ll show up”

In that, King was more right than he probably knew. On April 10, 2015, an official release was published which resulted in the film that premiered in 2017:

“Sony Pictures has teamed with MRC to co-finance *The Dark Tower*. Sony will distribute what is planned to be the first in a series of movies. A complementary TV series is also being developed by MRC.”

On his part, Stephen King stated:

“Sony Pictures has teamed with MRC to co-finance *The Dark Tower*. Sony will distribute what is planned to be the first in a series of movies. A complementary TV series is also being developed by MRC.”

Things now began moving quickly. Nicolaj Arcel was attached to direct, a release date for the film was set as January 13, 2017, and

Matthew McConaughey was contracted. Rumor has it that he was allowed to choose whether to play Roland or Randall Flagg. Regardless of whether he chose or not, in the film he plays Flagg. Idris Elba was cast as Roland, a choice satisfying to far from all. In the books, Roland is described as a gunslinger similar to Clint Eastwood, and now instead a black man had been cast to play him. Many were irked at this, but let us disregard those who hold something against black persons, which is simply stupid. However, casting a black actor as Roland does create problems with the plot of the novels, since anyone who has read them will know that when the Detta Walker character appears, she is not just a black person but one who holds neither trusts nor can stand Roland for being white. This conflict, which is central to the story until finally resolved, is something which would have to be handled differently after the decision to cast Elba.

Discussions were rampant on the Internet. King himself seemed less concerned than many of his constant readers:

"To me, the color of the gunslinger doesn't matter. What I care about is how fast he can draw...and that he takes care of the ka-tet"

Let's jump forward to May 3, 2017, when we had a first look at Roland, Jake, and Flagg as they appear in the film. Opinions were, to put it mildly, mixed. A new release date for the film was set as August 4, 2017, but before than a second trailer was released on July 10. On July 17, only two and a half weeks before the premiere, it was announced that the movie would have a run time of 95 minutes. Really? How could the story possibly be told that briefly? After a third trailer, and a statement where director Nokolaj Arcel claimed that this film was only the beginning of a series, the premiere date finally arrived, and more than ten years after the first rumors about the books being slated for filming the film turned out to be a total disaster. With very few exceptions, Stephen King enthusiasts hated the film, which had made the mistake of trying to satisfy dyed-in-the-wool King readers while at the same time attracting audiences who had no idea of what ”The Dark Tower” series was, a thing impossible to do in an hour and a half. Twelve days after the premiere, Nikolaj Arcel stated publicly that he would have no connection with any possible further Dark Tower films.

There is no need to further discuss the 2017 film here. If you want to watch it, or read the in most cases scathing reviews, you are welcome to do so on your own. But I do want to focus briefly on the fact that it did not mean the end of the chances for ”The Dark Tower” series to be filmed.

Already on the same day as the film premiered, Augusti 4, 2017, a rumor appeared claiming that Glen Mazzara, who had previously been the show runner for *The Walking Dead* TV series, would have the same function in a TV series based on ”The Dark Tower” books. When I asked him, Mazzara confirmed the rumor, but what did it in fact mean? Would such a series build on the film, or would everyone just forget about the movie and start over? At the time, nobody seemed to know, but in January, 2018, new information appeared stating that filming would being during the Summer of 2018 in England as well as in Ireland, and that none of the actors from the film would reprise their roles. A month later it became known that Amazon had bought rights to a huge number of possible sources for future TV shows: J. R. R. Tolkien's *The Lord of the Rings*, Robert Jordan's *The Wheel of Time*, Neal Stephenson's *Snow Crash* … and ”The Dark Tower” book series.

In February, 2019, Amazon announced that it had decided to go on with a ”Dark Tower” series. The first season would consist of 13 one hour episodes, and Mazzara was still the show runner. But it was also decided that the series would have to wait for some time, in order to premiere more distantly from the then less than two years old movie, which had been both a critical and financial fiasco. In March, nevertheless, the company announced which actors had been retained to play the main characters. Sam Strike would be Roland, Jasper Rääkkönen would be Martin, The Man in Black. It was also disclosed that filming would start with the fourth book in the series, *Wizard and Glass*. A month later, Jerome Flynn (who played Bronn in *A Game of Thrones*) was confirmed as Roland's father Steven Deschain; two months later, we also learned that Joana Ribeiro would play Roland's first love, Susan Delgado, and the first photos from the production, which had begun in Croatia, were published. This was true happiness! At long last, we would be treated to a genuine filmed version of Stephen King's books. Or so we believed. But on January 2020, Amazon instead disclosed that it had abandoned its "The Dark Tower" series, despite the pilot segment having been finished. The reason, according to the company, was that it was felt that the pilot was not grand enough for a major investment, and therefore instead the company would go ahead with its proposed serials based on *The Wheel of Time* and *The Lord of the Rings*.

Suddenly we had arrived at a point where a pilot segment had been recorded but would never be shown. This was total frustration. And adding insult to injury, Mazzara disclosed his plans for the proposed first three seasons, which seemed very promising indeed:

"Season One ended with the death of Susan. In Season 2, the war with Farson is building. I was maybe going to use the shapeshifter story [from *Wind Through the Keyhole*] as part of season 2, and get to the death of Gabrielle and either the fall of Gilead there or the fall of Gilead would be the season three premiere. Very quickly, there would be a last stand at Jericho Hill and by episode 3.03 or 3.04 I was going to have Roland stumble out into the desert, follow him into the desert and then I was going to do a time-lapse so that maybe you actually age Roland and switch actors. Then you have a new Roland reset the show at the top of season three, then go into *The Gunslinger* and by the end of that season go into *The Drawing of the Three*."

Most people will never get the chance to see Amazon's pilot episode. I am one of the lucky ones who have seen it and, in addition, have read the manuscripts for the first six episodes of the first season. Let me briefly comment on some things in it.

One noticeable thing is that Mazzara has obviously planned ahead. In the manuscript, there are numerous notes about things to come in later episodes or seasons. Among these I noted one reference to Mia's presence in the banquet hall of Castle Discordia. In episode two, Roland and his friends discover a thinny (a place where the border between worlds has been almost obliterated) and we can read:

The WHINE is louder now but they still can't determine its source. It's an eerie, off-putting, strangely melodious TWANG. When EDDIE DEAN hears it in Season 5, he'll say:

EDDIE
Sounds Hawaiian, doesn't it?
But that's another story.

Or in other words, we see that Mazzara already here is planning for Eddie to enter the story and how he will react to the sound from a thinny in an episode four seasons in the future.

Another change is in who belongs to Roland's original ka-tet. In the books, in Roland's youth, his ka-tet consists of Cuthbert Allgood, Alain Johns, and Jamie DeCurry. They are all also in the series, though Mazzara's manuscript makes Jamie a woman, which was not the case in the novel, and a fourth character has been added: Aileen Ritter.

Cuthbert Allgood is portrayed by Khalil Madovi, and in the books he is described as Roland's best childhood friend, and is often called just Bert. We meet him for the first time already in the first book in the series, *The Gunslinger*, but he plays no major role until the fourth book, *Wizard and Glass*. Both in the books and in the script his favorite weapon is a slingshot. Cuthbert and Alain are the two friends who follow Roland to Mejis in the fourth book.

Alain Johns is played by Frankie Fox, and in the serial has the power of influencing persons with his ”touch”; in that way, he is able to make them obey his wishes. Jamie DeCurry is played by Joanna McGibbon, and as mentioned this is a character whose gender has been changed from the books, where Jamie figures most prominently in *The Wind Through the Keyhole*, the late addition to the series, where he travels with Roland to investigate a violent attack in a nearby town.

One character who has been given a much larger role than she had in Stephen King's books is Ileen Ritter, whose first name in the books was spelled Aileen. In the books she was not part of Roland's original ka-tet, but his teacher Curt's niece and Roland's intended bride. Curt brings her up after her parents are killed while on a leisure trip to Cressia, and covertly teaches her when she becomes obsessed by the idea of becoming a gunslinger. Though a female gunslinger is unthinkable in the Gilead of the books, she begins dressing as a boy, frees Roland from prison and escapes with him, thus surviving the fall of Gilead, performs heroically during the battle of Jericho Hill, but is mortally wounded and dies while returning with Roland to Gilead. Possibly letting her survive to be part of the much later story told in "The Dark Tower" series is intended to give her the chance of finally being a true woman gunslinger.

Based on what I have seen and read of the series, I believe that it would have been both impressive and true to the books. At least judging from the first few episodes it seems as if Mazzara had a clear and consistent notion of how to bring his series all the way through Roland's quest. But unfortunately we will never know, since Amazon pulled out of the series and no other production company picked it up.

At that point, it again seemed as if the perennial story of filming "The Dark Tower" had ended. But no. A little less than three years after Amazon bid the notion adieu, on December 8, 2022, the news broke that Mike Flanagan, who has written, directed and in at least one case also produced such earlier Stephen King features as *Gerald's Game* (2017), *Doctor Sleep* (2019), and *Life of Chuck* (2024) now owns the rights to "The Dark Tower" series. Flanagan said that he envisioned a five season TV series and two standalone feature films (haven't we heard that before?), and again the hopefulness I believed had finally been put to sleep rears its head. Is it possible that after all we will finally get that ultimate filmed version? Well, perhaps. At this writing, early in 2025, there has still been no updates, nor any news about who has been cast as who. So eighteen years after the first news of the books being set for filming, we again simply have to wait and see.

Interlude 5: About a cover

Never judge a book by its cover. How often have you heard someone say that? In most cases it is true, but at the same time it is a difficult thing to do. After all, the cover is the first thing you see when you look at a book, online or in a store, and often the cover is the reason you pick a particular book up from a display table. But why does a book get the specific cover it has? Why does the same book have so widely different covers depending on in which country it happens to be published – or even depending on whether it is a hardcover book or a paperback reprint in the same country?

Many factors play into this. What kind of covers are popular at a particular time? What dominant colors are assumed to attract attention? What do customers seem to like best in a particular market segment? Do you have inhouse illustrators you want to use, are you free to have covers made by freelancers, or are you limited to buying reprint rights to some already existing illustration? Many choices have to be made, and all of them will influence the final cover.

But sometimes the author may make all those decisions. This was what happened with the cover illustration on the original hardcover edition of Stephen King's novel *Under the Dome* (Scribner, 2009). He asked a design company called Platinum to create a cover for his book, even sending along a sketch outlining how he visualized it. And from that sketch Platinum created one of the most impressive covers ever to adorn a Stephen King book.

An interview with Platinum

When I first saw the cover of *Under the Dome*, I though it one of the most attractive covers on a Stephen King book I had ever seen. It made me wonder about what makes a cover look the way it does. To find out, I got in touch with Platinum in Rio de Janeiro, Brazil, who had designed the cover for *Under the Dome*. And on November 11, 2009, I learned more about how the cover had been created, and was also told that King himself had provided a sketch of how he wanted the cover to look.

Platinum is an Image Concept Studio which uses all available artistic means in order to find the best solution to construct images. And that is exactly what they have done with the cover for King's book *Under the Dome*. I got to talk to the people involved in the cover and they also showed me some images that illustrate how the cover evolved from King's first sketch to the finished cover.

Lilja: How did Platinum get involved with the cover for *Under the Dome*?

Platinum team: We received an email from our agent in New York saying that Mr. King himself wanted us to create the cover for *Under the Dome*. As it turns out he is a fan of Platinum. We could hardly believe it, especially because some of us are huge fans of him.

Lilja: Judging from King's sketch the basic idea for the cover came directly from him?

Platinum team: Yes, he drew a rough sketch of what was on his mind. It's never an easy job to interpret someone else's drawings but Mr. King's was a bit more challenging. When we first got the image we all thought there was a man in front of the dome, later we found out it was a dog. It was funny but I think that in the end we got the idea.

Lilja: Did you get to read the book before designing the cover or did you just know the basics of what should be included on the cover itself?

Platinum team: We got his manuscripts without the ending. We read it and discussed how to enrich the basic idea. Platinum images are always filled with details. It's kind of our trademark. And because it was Mr. King's book, we tried to use key elements about the story without revealing it, to keep the mystery and entice the readers.

Lilja: Can you take me through the process that followed on King's first sketch and eventually to the finished cover?

Platinum team: We received the first sketch and sat down with our illustrator to come up with a few drawings as options. We sent them back and they chose one. Then we started working on the concept itself, which is not the cover yet, it's just a drawing with all the elements. Then it went back to the client and once it was approved we started working on the final cover. It changed a lot in this process. At first the dome would fit just in the front cover but our illustrator had the idea to use only half of the dome, they loved it so much that they decided to do the dome from flap to flap.

Lilja: Was King involved through the entire process or did you just show him the final art for approval?

Platinum team: He was very involved. He asked for a few changes and was open to our suggestions. It was easy working with him. He knew what he wanted and I think there were chemistry throughout this process. We captured his vision but, as our agent likes to say, we "platinumized it".

Lilja: The different stages of the cover look quite different even though the basic idea is there in all of them. How did the discussions go that made you make the changes that led to the finished version?

Platinum team: We have ideas all the time, even after we have a final concept, and we are always trying to improve what we have. Why not?

Lilja: Especially image five and six are very much alike but at the same time not. What convinced you those changes were the right once?

Platinum team: The difference in these two happened when one of us said that the front cover could look like an ordinary day, but when you turn to the back cover you would see a lot going on. It was just an idea but we decided to go for it and see how it would work. We liked it so we suggested it to the client. They liked it as well. This is how the process goes. We have ideas and we try them, some work, others don't. It's always a work in progress until the end.

Lilja: There was a lot of secrecy surrounding the cover before it was revealed. Did you feel anything of that? Did people try to get you to reveal it ahead of time?

Platinum team: The publisher was careful enough not to reveal our name before the final revealing. We know that the art director received emails from fans on his personal account but not us.

Lilja: Was working on a Stephen King (who is a big selling author) cover different from you other work?

Platinum team: Yes. We usually work with advertisement. We are used to working with big clients and big accounts all over the world, but Stephen King was different because he is an icon. It was a mix of anxiety and excitement.

Lilja: What kind of response have you had about the cover?

Platinum team: Everyone loved it and the thing about this project is that it's not an ad in a magazine or on an outdoor poster board. It's Stephen King and he has a lot of diehard fans who will analyze and scrutinize this image. I read one of his fans commenting on his website something about the position of the stars. He had a very interesting theory about them. Unfortunately, the position was completely random. But this just gives an idea of how great a responsibility it is. And we are very proud of it.

Lilja: Is there anything about working on the cover, or about the cover itself, that you would like to mention to all the King fans out there reading this? Will you read the book if you haven't?

Platinum team: We still don't know the ending! Can you believe it? We are anxiously waiting for our copies. They are on their way here to Brazil. To the fans we would like to say that we were very honored to work with Mr. King. This was definitely not an ordinary project but we had good times doing it. We hope you enjoy it as much as we do.

Lilja: OK, thank you all for taking the time to answer my questions. It was a lot of fun!

The Shop

Stephen King is known for recycling his characters, but he also uses both locations and organizations repeatedly in many both short stories and novels. One example is The Shop, or more correctly, The Department of Scientific Intelligence, as it is formally called. Much of the history of this organization is secret, but it is known that it in 1969 performed an experiment with a chemical code named ”Lot Six”. The man in charge of these experiments was Dr. Joseph Wanless, who worked at The Shop as head psychologist. He has been described as overweight, with thinning hair and small, pink fingers. He wore small, rimless eyeglasses and a laboratory coat and made a habit of crumbling his cigarettes. After a stroke, the left corner of his mouth is hanging down as in a sneer, his left hand is twisted into a claw and he spoke in a soft, croaking voice. He walked with a stick. Dr. Wanless was called The Mad Doctor.

On May 11, 1969, Dr. Joseph Wanless arrived at Harrison State College to perform his ”Lot Six” experiment. Twelve students volunteered and half of them would be injected with ”Lot Six” while the other half would be given distilled water. A double-blind method was used, meaning that neither the scientists nor the students knew who was given what. After having been injected the students were observed for 48 hours. Two lab assistants handed out forms with 25 yes–no questions to the students before the start of the experiment. Some of the questions read:

- Have you ever had psychiatric counseling?
- Do you believe that you have ever had an authentic psychic experience?
- Have you ever used any hallucinogenic drug?
- Have you ever had a fracture or a serious sprain?

- Two of the students were Andrew McGee and Victoria Tomlinson. They would later become the parents of Charlie McGee.
- The experiment was performed in room 70 in The Jason Gearneigh Hall. Staff from The Shop pretended to be lab assistants, and it turned out that all twelve students were injected with ”Lot Six”. The result was disastrous:
- Test person #1 died from cardiac arrest during the experiment.
- Test person #2 died shortly after the test in his dormitory, possibly from cerebral embolism.
- Test person #3 went insane, clawed their own eyes out and is confined in a facility in Maui.
- Test person #4 went insane, suffered from psychotic paralysis and is confined in a facility in Maui.
- Test person #5 died in a car accident in 1972.
- Test person #6 jumped from the roof of the Cleveland Post Office in 1973.
- Test persons #7, #8, and #9 all committed suicide from 1974 through 1977.
- Test person £10 was James Richardson. Immediately after the experiment, he displayed significant psychic abilities, similar to those Carrie White had possessed. He is currently living in Los Angeles, and whether he still retains any psychokinetic abilities is unknown.
- Test person #11 was Andrew McGee. He was later killed by John Rainbird.
- Test person #12 was Victoria Tomlinson. She was later killed by The Shop.

Dr. Wanless had also worked on further chemical combinations called ”Lot Seven” and ”Lot Eight”, but given the outcome of the ”Lot Six” test, work on these was halted.

Over the years, we have become acquainted with a number of individuals all working for The Shop. Let me introduce you to them.

John Rainbird (in *Firestarter*)

Some of those employed by The Shop have distinguished themselves more than others. One of those is John Rainbird, a Native American who works for The Shop as an agent and assassin and who is a badly scarred Vietnam veteran. He is also a psychopath obsessed with the afterlife and with what happens when someone dies. This he tries to discern by looking into the eyes of his victims as they die. He also believes that this bestows on him a power he wants to bring along when his turn comes to pass into the realms of the dead. When he becomes aware of Charlie McGee and learns what she is capable of, he becomes convinced that her death will gift him with special abilities which he wants to possess and bring with him to his afterlife.

It is Rainbird who kills both Andy McGee and Dr. Wanless, but when he tries to kill Charlie McGee he fails. Instead she kills both him and James ”Cap” Hollister by setting fire to them.

Captain James Hollister (in *Firestarter* and ”The Mist”)

Hollister, also called just ”Cap”, is one of the highest ranking at The Shop. He is ruthless and uses murder as a method of accomplishing his goals. If necessary, even his own associates are killed. After having learned what special wild talents Charlie McGee has, he wants to use them for military purposes. If he can use her as a weapon, he can obliterate all enemies of the United States. It is also Hollister who recruits John Rainbird to The Shop, an act he later comes to regret when he realizes that Rainbird is insane and that it is because of him Hollister himself is set on fire by Charlie.

In the 2022 remake of the film made from *Firestarter*, Hollister has turned into a woman and is now named Jane Hollister.

Joseph Wanless (in *Firestarter*)

Wanless was responsible for the ”Lot Six” experiments and was never able to let them go. On August 8, 1974, the same day Richard Nixon announced his resignation as President, Wanless had a stroke from which he never entirely recuperated. Instead he grew steadily more obsessed by his experiment and the students involved. In August, 1980, he managed to get The Shop to capture the McGee family. Vicky was tortured to death and Charlie was kidnapped, later to be saved by his father but then recaptured. Although The Shop wanted to use Charlie as a weapon, Wanless wanted both her and Andy to be killed, since he realized how great a threat to the entire world Charlie might become. However, Captain Hollister did not agree with him and instead considered Wanless insane. So in the end, Hollister sent Rainbird to Room 1217 at the Mayflower Hotel in Washington, D.C., with orders to kill Wanless. Rainbird strangled him with his bare hands.

Orville Jamieson (in *Firestarter*)

One of The Shop’s agents. Together with John Mayo he hunts Andy and Charlie. He prefers to be called ”OJ” or ”The Juice”. Carries a .357 Magnum, which he calls ”The Windsucker”.

John Mayo (in *Firestarter*)

Another agent for The Shop, now together with Orville Jamieson hunting Andy and Charlie. Mayo and Norville Bates both posed as assistants during Dr. Wanless ”Lot Six” experiment.

Dr. Herman Pynchot (in *Firestarter*)

One of the three physicians at The Shop. He experimented on both Andy and Charlie, and was the one too convinced Charlie that she would be allowed to see her father if she only does as she is told. But she never sees him.

Al Steinowitz (in *Firestarter*)

One of The Shop's agents. He takes part in hunting for Andy and Charlie.

Norville Bates (in *Firestarter*)

Another agent of The Shop hunting Andy and Charlie. He shows a photo of them to a policeman at the airport and is told how the shoes of a soldier, Eddie Delgrado, inexplicably began burning. Bates along with John Mayo posed as assistants during Dr. Wanless' "Lot Six" experiments.

Ralph Baxter (in *Firestarter*)

An ex-CIA official now working for The Shop. In his career he has killed three men and one woman. He also raped the woman after having killed her. He, too, took part in Dr. Wanless' experiments, injecting the test persons with their doses of "Lot Six".

Jude Andrews (in *Golden Years*)

Jude Andrews is an agent for The Shop. He is sent after Harlan and Gina Williams after Harlan by mistake has been subjected to an experiment making him grow continuously younger.

In addition to appearing in *Firestarter* and *Golden Years*, The Shop is mentioned in three other stories by Stephen King:

- "The Langoliers": Those surviving the interdimensional jump wonder if they may be unwitting subjects to some experiment performed by The Shop or some similar organization.

- *The Stand*: There is a discussion of whether it might have been possible to capture Charles D. Campion before he reached Texas, if The Shop had immediately been given the task.

- *The Tommyknockers*: The Shop is mentioned as being interested in what Andersson and Gard have found buried in the ground.

By now, it's quite a while since Stephen King referred to The Shop in his fiction. We can wonder why. Perhaps it no longer feels as topical. Or perhaps it just doesn't fit anywhere in the later books and stories. Personally I admit that I would happily see a novel *about* The Shop and its origins.

It is the tale, not he who tells it

In both "The Breathing Method" (in *Different Seasons*, Viking, 1982) and "The Man Who Would Not Shake Hands" (in *Skeleton Crew*, Putnam, 1985), Stephen King writes about a secret club impossible to visit unless you are a member. In "The Breathing Method", lawyer David Adley visits the club and gets to hear the story of pregnant Sandra Stansfield. In "The Man Who Would Not Shake Hands" it is George Gregson who tells the story of Henry Brower, the man who refused to shake hands. In this story as well, David Adley is present.

So what kind of a club is this? It has no name, and so is only called "The Club". It is situated on 249 East 35th Street on Manhattan, and the butler's name is Stevens, who has worked as the club butler for innumerable years. The purpose of the club itself is to convey stories. Over the large fireplace you can read the club's motto: "It is the tale, not he who tells it". Members come to hear stories, and every evening one or more members will tell one. The last Thursday before Christmas is set aside for horror stories.

Stephen King's The Club has an enormous library full of books who do not exist, written by non-existing authors and published by companies that have never been. Additionally, at least according to Stevens, the butler, there are many entrances and exits to and from the club, a claim which has made many readers believe that The Club may have something to do with The Dark Tower. At the end of "The Breathing Method", David Adley reflects,

"and when the wind rose in another wild whoop, I felt momentarily sure that the front door would blow open, revealing not 35th Street but an insane Clark Ashton Smith landscape where the bitter shapes of twisted trees stood silhouetted on a sterile horizon below which double suns were setting in a gruesome red glare."

"I opened my mouth. And the question that came out was: 'Are there many more rooms upstairs?'

'Oh, yes, sir,' he said, his eyes never leaving mine. 'A great many. A man could become lost. In fact, men *have* become lost. Sometimes it seems to me that they go on for miles. Rooms and corridors.'

'And entrances and exits?'

His eyebrows went up slightly. 'Oh yes. Entrances and exits.'"

This suggests that some of The Club's door open on other worlds, and we know that such doors exist also in The Dark Tower stories. But this is pure speculation; King himself has never confirmed it.

Does The Club actually exist? Probably not, but its address certainly does, and at 249 East 35th Street, New York, NY 10016, there is a four-story house built in 1920. Officially it houses the Permanent Mission of Malta to the United Nations, which according to its Internet site is the diplomatic mission to the UN of the Republic of Malta and works to promote peace, justice, and progress for all:

> *Welcome to the website of the Permanent Mission of Malta to the United Nations in New York. I hope that you will find this website a useful introduction to the work of the Mission on the wide range of issues it covers in pursuit of Malta's Foreign Policy objectives.*
> *The Permanent Mission works within the United Nations to advance Malta's interests and uphold its values. Together with other Member States Malta seeks to address challenges of the 21st Century. In so doing, we strive to promote peace,*

justice and prosperity for all by building a stronger United Nations whose actions will succeed in improving the lives of present as well as future generations.

Whether this is actually just a cover for a secret Club I leave up to every reader to decide on their own. Personally I took a detour there on my last visit to New York City. I considered knocking on the door but in the end decided against it …

Interlude 6: Cujo

Someone whose professional life as an actor and stunt man has sometimes probably been more both bizarre and demanding than he had foreseen is Gary Morgan. And particularly demanding (as well as bizarre) was probably his role in the film version of *Cujo* (1983). Most probably almost everyone who has seen the film even missed his contributions to entirely, since Gary Morgan is the actor who in some scenes plays Cujo himself. Of course the character was also portrayed by actual dogs: Five St. Bernards (one of them named Daddy) and one black Labrador Retriever took turns playing Cujo with Gary Morgan and a specially built mechanical dog's head. If you'd only known when you saw the movie.

Incidentally, there is a fun photograph where Dee Wallace, who played Donna, the woman who is trapped with her son in her car by Cujo, Gary Morgan, and Lewis Teague, the film's director, dancing together. You'll find it on the Internet if you search for "Dancing Cujo".

An interview with Frank Darabont

During a period of fifteen months, during 2007 and 2008, I had the opportunity of talking a few times with Frank Darabont, the director of one short and three feature films based on Stephen King stories: *The Woman in the Room* (1983), the Oscar nominee *The Shawshank Redemption* (1994), *The Green Mile* (1999), and *The Mist* (2007). When the first interview was recorded, on February 6, 2007, Darabont was just on the verge of filming *The Mist*, but the conversation focused on how it all began and didn't go on to discuss that movie. Darabont was very open about his beginnings in the film business and how he became one of the most highly regarded directors of Stephen King films.

Lilja: First, let me thank you for agreeing to this interview. It's a real honor!

Frank Darabont: Thanks for having me!

Lilja: In 1983 you did *The Woman in the Room*. Can you tell me how that happened? As I understand it's one of the first Dollar Babies, right?

Frank Darabont: In 1980, I was 20 years old, working many miserable low-paid jobs just to survive and dreaming of a career in films someday. During that time I was a theater usher, telephone operator … man, I can't even remember all the awful jobs I had back then. I even ran a forklift and did a lot of heavy lifting for an auction company that liquidated industrial machine shops. That was the year I approached Stephen King about "The Woman in the Room", and I hadn't even had my first job in movies yet! But I nonetheless decided I wanted to make a short film from his story, which I thought was lovely and deeply moving, so I wrote him a letter asking for his permission. I was shocked that he said yes. (I found out later about his "dollar baby" policy, which shows what a generous man he is. I doubt *The Woman in the Room* was the first dollar baby, but I'm certain it must be among the first wave of those films.)

Let me digress to say that my very first real job in films happened later that same year, after I'd gotten Steve's permission to do *The Woman in the Room*. Chuck Russell hired me as a P.A. on a shitty no-budget film called *Hell Night*, starring Linda Blair. If you haven't seen it, I don't really recommend it. Quentin Tarantino keeps telling me he really likes *Hell Night*, but I keep telling him he's the only one. It was one of the cheesier entries in the "slasher movie" cycle. But if you ever do see it, you can check out my name in the end credits – my very first movie job! "P.A.," by the way, stands for "production assistant," although I've always felt it could also stand for "pissant." It is the lowest job in movies, a gofer who runs around doing every crappy job they hand you and never getting any sleep. I made 150 dollars a week, which was horrible pay even back then. But it was my entry into the film business, and began my association with Chuck Russell. Chuck was a line producer on low budget films at that time, just making a living, which is how he hired me. We later became dear friends and wound up collaborating as writers on a number of screenplays, including *A Nightmare on Elm Street 3: Dream Warriors*. That was Chuck's first directing job and my first professional writing credit, in 1986.

Anyway, back to 1980. I wrote Steve King my letter, he said yes, and it took me three years to make *The Woman in the Room*. It took a while to raise enough money (from some kindly investors in Iowa) to shoot the movie and get it in the can. But then I had to personally earn the rest of the money needed to put the film through post-production: editing the film, doing the sound, paying for the lab work, etc. By 1983 I was working as a prop assistant on TV commercials – not great money, but it was enough to get my movie finished. I earned $11,000 dollars that year and spent $7,000 of it finishing my movie – how I survived on $4,000 that year is something I still can't explain; to this day I have no idea how I did it. (The IRS was also quite curious … that was the only year I've ever gotten audited for taxes, because they couldn't believe anybody could survive on $4,000 a year.) All I can say is, my rent was cheap and I lived very frugally. I spent that entire year with a borrowed Moviola in my bedroom, editing the film. I had heaps of 16 mm film piled all over the place. At night, I had to move all the piles of film off my bed onto the floor so I could go to sleep. In the morning, I'd have to move the piles of film from the floor back onto my bed so I could walk to the bathroom. Very glamorous!

But eventually the movie did get done, and we entered it for Oscar consideration in the short film category. There are two things we should correct: 1) It wasn't the 1986 Academy Awards, but earlier – either '83 or '84, I forget the exact year. 2) More significantly, *The Woman in the Room* was not nominated … it was named in the top 9 out of the 90 short films submitted that year, but we failed to make the final cut of 4 nominated films. (For some strange reason, the common belief has arisen through the years that the film was nominated, but that is incorrect.)

Lilja: Did King comment on what he thought about it? *The Woman in the Room* is a rather personal story to him.. .

Frank Darabont: He liked it. In fact, we used his quote "Clearly the best of the short films made from my stuff" on the video box. He did feel the character I added, The Prisoner (played by Brian Libby, who later played Floyd in The *Shawshank Redemption*) was a bit cliched, and I can't disagree. Steve's favorite bit was the dream sequence where the mom turns into a rotted corpse – he loved that! Hey, give Steve a rotted corpse and he's your pal for life. Here's some trivia: that corpse originally appeared in *Hell Night*. (If I remember correctly, Linda Blair stumbles into a room at one point where a bunch of corpses are propped around a table – it was a male corpse, but in my short I passed him off as a woman. Corpse in drag!) Some two years after *Hell Night*, I borrowed the corpse to use in *The Woman in the Room* from the makeup fx guys who built it. He wound up sitting in my living room for a few months. Sometimes I'd wake up in the middle of the night and forget he was there. I'd wander half-asleep out to the kitchen to get a glass of water and he'd scare the shit out of me, this big human shape sitting in the dark in my living room.

That dream sequence was something I also added to the story – looking back on it, I guess I took a lot of liberties with Steve's material. I'm kind of surprised he liked it as much as he did. But he liked it well enough that when I approached him again in 1986 to ask for the rights to *The Shawshank Redemption*, he said yes. So spending three years busting my ass to make that short did pay off in a very nice way. It gave Steve a certain amount of confidence in me.

As for me, I look at *The Woman in the Room* now and wonder what Steve saw in it. The movie actually makes me cringe a little, as I suppose any work you did as a kid will make you cringe (unless you're Mozart). Honestly, it looks like an earnest but very young filmmaker at work to me. The result strikes me as pretty creaky and overly careful in its approach. I think I was really afraid of making any mistakes, so my approach to shooting and editing was cautious, to say the least. And it's slow! Yikes!

Lilja: He later gave the OK to put it out on video. Who's idea was that? Yours? King's? Most Dollar Babies never reach any wide audience, so it must have felt good.

Frank Darabont: That was always my intention, even when I first approached him for the rights. So, yes, I was a dollar baby in a sense, but I had worked out a deal with his agent that paid Steve some more money if I got video distribution. So he eventually made more than a buck, though it was still a very generous deal for us. Unfortunately, the video distributor we originally got into business with totally fucked us. The guy's name was Gary Gray (not the director, I hasten to add!), this bottom-feeder with no integrity who made a shitload of money on the video but never paid us a dime of it, even though we had signed contracts. Jeff Shiro, who made *The Boogeyman* (which was paired with *The Woman in the Room* on the video), got equally screwed. Of course I didn't have a dime to my name back then, so hiring a lawyer was out of the question. I don't know if Gray is still out there somewhere, but I bet he is. Any young filmmakers thinking of getting into business with him should run in the opposite direction. And Gary, if you're reading this: shame on you. I may track you down and come after you some day with a tribe of high-priced Hollywood lawyers shrieking like crazed Apaches in an old Western, just to see the look on your face.

At some point along the way, the video got bought by Spelling's video releasing company. I'm not even sure how that happened. I imagine it was that original distributor trying to squeeze a few more bucks out of it. Happily, Spelling did have integrity, they do business in a straightforward manner, so money started trickling in for a few years. It was a pleasure all those years later to track down my Iowa investors and send them checks. That's all I ever wanted, to see them paid back. It took a while, but at least they got their money. I think I might have kicked in a few bucks of my own, since I was making a good living by then.

Lilja: Then 11 years later you did *The Shawshank Redemption*, which became a huge success and was nominated for seven Academy Awards. It's also one of the most popular adaptations from a King story. Why do you think that is?

Frank Darabont: Well, it's the power of the story, for sure. Steve wrote a humdinger there, he hit that ball right over the fence. It has a tremendous humanity to it, which makes for the best kind of storytelling. I recognized it the moment I read it. And it works gorgeously as a metaphor – everybody who sees it can project their own trials and tribulations, and hopes for triumph, into it. I've often referred to it as the "Rorshach Test" of movies. People see what they want to see in it, even if they've never been to prison. It's a very potent experience that way, and that's all credit to Steve King. The man writes deep, and with that story he was writing deeper than usual. All I had to do was translate it to the screen and not screw it up. I'm probably making that sound easier than it was, but the task was made a lot easier by the fact that I had Castle Rock's complete trust and support. That's an amazing group of people at that company. Bless their hearts, because the level of trust a filmmaker experiences there is almost unique in this business. If I'd had standard studio interference and meddling on that movie, if I'd spent my time battling to defend my film against executives who wanted everything different, Lord knows how that movie would have turned out. Probably not so well. It would have been some crappy prison movie long forgotten by now. But I had Castle Rock, and they were just the best.

Lilja: How happy are you with that movie yourself? Is it fair to say that *The Shawshank Redemption* was your big break?

Frank Darabont: I'd certainly qualify *The Shawshank Redemption* as a big break. You can't get seven Academy Award nominations including Best Picture and not suddenly be taken very seriously as a director. And that movie led directly to *The Green Mile*. Hanks, one of my favorite people in the world, saw *The Shawshank Redemption* and rang me up and said: "Hey, love your work, we should find something to do together. If you ever have a script you think I'd be right for, send it to me." That's quite a nice door to have opened.

And, yes, I'm delighted with the movie. I watched it again when we had our 10 Year Anniversary screening and DVD re-release about two years ago. And with all that time and distance, I was knocked out by how well the movie holds up. (I'm glad I didn't get the same feeling I got watching *The Woman in the Room* again!) You know, after a decade goes by, you (the filmmaker) don't really feel like you had anything to do with it, you just kind of sit there and watch the movie on its own terms. It's almost like somebody else's movie by then, you just get caught up in the story like any audience member. And I was very pleased with what I saw. It's that Steve King tale, man, it works a treat. But the thing that really jumped out at me was how great Tim Robbins was. I'd somewhat forgotten that. Everybody talks about Morgan Freeman, and of course he's just superb … I always hear how much everybody loves his narration … but Tim really carries equal weight on his shoulders for the movie working so well, truly. Don't tell him I said that, he'll get a swelled head.

Lilja: Then five years later you have another success based on a King book. This time it's *The Green Mile*, which was nominated for four Academy Awards. Why do you think your King adaptations are so successful?

Frank Darabont: Because when I recognize that a story is great, I try not to mess with it too much. I promise you, that's not a glib answer. That's why *The Green Mile* wound up being three hours long. I'm the first to admit that's not an optimal length for a movie … it's a lot to ask of an audience to sit for three hours...but if I'd made that movie two hours, it would have cut the heart out of Steve's story. It would have given us a mangled version.

Lilja: Just the other day I was listening to your commentary track for *The Green Mile*. Just how hard was it to talk for 3 hours straight?

Frank Darabont: That's when I swore I'd never make another three hour movie again! Sitting in that recording booth! We joked about that quite a lot. I swear, trying to keep commentary fresh for that long is a challenge. And I'm not one of these guys who just mumbles through a commentary and doesn't care if it's good or not, or if there are long gaps of silence. To me, it all has to be right, or I shouldn't be doing it. The way I figure, if you buy my DVD and are willing to give me three hours of your life to hear what I have to say, I better damn well say something worth your time and money.

So I think I might have set a record for time spent recording a commentary. Call the Guinness Book. The whole process, beginning to end, was about nine months. I don't mean nine months putting the DVD together, I'm talking nine months recording that commentary track alone. Of course I wasn't in there every day, but I did devote every day that I could spare out of my schedule. We should have kept a log of hours to say for sure, but I'm betting if we total it all up it's about three or four solid weeks of full-time work: recording commentary, working with the editor (giving him endless notes) to lay it in the right way, re-recording sections if they sucked the first time, re-editing to accommodate that, going back and filling in all the gaps and silences. I'm told most directors spend an afternoon or two in the recording booth, but I spent the better part of a year. I'm the first to admit that's excessive, but I figure it's my time and I want to do the job right. As I said, I owe the listener my best effort.

I have to say, the fine folks at Warner Video were really patient. I'm sure they were tearing their hair out, but they never showed it. At least not to me.

Lilja: All three King movies you have done so far have been nominated for Academy Awards (*The Woman in the Room* was nominated in 1986 as best short film). Do you feel an Oscar-pressure with *The Mist*?

Frank Darabont: Again, let's clarify that *The Woman in the Room* wasn't nominated. That's a myth. I suppose I could just keep my mouth shut about it and let people think I'm cooler than I am, but that's just not in my vocabulary. Fair is fair, and it wouldn't be fair to the people whose films were nominated.

As for *The Mist*, no. I feel absolutely no Oscar pressure, because there's no way it'll be nominated for anything! It's just not that kind of movie! It's what I describe as a "nasty little gut-punch horror flick," and those just aren't on the Oscar radar at all. The only pressure I feel is to get the movie done on such a tight schedule and tight budget – it's a real nut-cruncher from that standpoint. But I'm taking inspiration from Danny Boyle – he did *28 Days Later* with very limited resources, and that turned out great. He's my hero.

Well, then again, I suppose there is a slight chance for some nomination in the effects category, who knows? I'm sure my effects will be great, but we're not nearly as effects-heavy as the films that usually get nominated in that category, like *Pirates of the Caribbean* or something. Café FX will be doing my CGI, and they're wonderful. My buddy Guillermo Del Toro turned me onto them; they did his effects on *Pan's Labyrinth*. Which is an awesome film! A masterpiece! Everybody must see it! And Café's work was terrific.

Plus there's my pal Greg Nicotero of KNB Effects handling the makeup effects and designing end. Greg and I have been designing Steve King's "mist monsters" for months now, and having a blast! Greg's one of my best friends, I've known him for fifteen years, and we're both monster kids from childhood. We both grew up reading *Famous Monsters of Filmland* and seeing every bad black & white movie we could – and even some good ones. We've talked for years about wanting to design some cool monsters together. Now we've gotten our chance, and I think we've come up with some fantastic and original designs. Greg's been just amazing. It helped quite a bit to have the legendary Bernie Wrightson, also a great friend, contributing some design ideas. There's a reason he's billed as The Master of the Macabre – he's awesome. Plus there are some other artists Greg uses in-house at KNB who contributed some wonderful stuff along the way – like this young guy named Mike Broom. He's a hell of an artist, and I think he has a big future.

Lilja: Will your adaptation of *The Mist* make use of the monsters that Stephen King describes?

Frank Darabont: It's all *about* the monsters! First: the monsters from another dimension that want to eat you. Second: the monsters you're trapped inside with, in this case your friends and neighbors you're trying to survive with, but who are going crazy with fear and pressure and might prove to be more dangerous than those hungry monsters outside. Like I said, it's a nasty little gut-punch horror flick, and one of those great pressure-cooker situations that King specializes in.

Lilja: I know you are working on more King movies and I wanted to ask you to comment on them, if you can. First out is of course *The Mist*. I know this one has been in the making for quite a long time and now you're finally ready to start filming. Can you tell me your plans for it and when we can expect to see it?

Frank Darabont: This one will be quite a change of pace for me … literally. It's a very tight budget and schedule, so it will be the fastest shooting I've yet done for a feature. I directed an episode of *The Shield* last year to prepare myself for this … a very fast and loose style, all handheld, very liberating for me in many ways. I'm not aware if *The Shield* has aired yet in other countries, so you may not be aware of it, but it's just terrific – one of my favorite shows ever, a very gritty police drama with amazing writing and an equally amazing cast. It makes *Hill Street Blues* or *NYPD Blue* look like *Sesame Street*. Its creator, Shawn Ryan, had been after me for a while to direct one because he knew what a big fan I am. Finally my schedule cleared and the opportunity was there, so I grabbed it. Doing the show was liberating, as I mentioned. Directing, for me, has always been a very precise and painstaking approach, like brain surgery. I jokingly call it "delusions of being Kubrick." Doing *The Shield* changed that aspect of it – it's very fast and loose, more like playing jazz than performing a precise classical composition. If what you're used to as a director is more like conducting a huge symphony orchestra performing Beethoven's Ninth in perfect tune, then suddenly shifting gears into jazz can be wonderful. It's throwing caution to the wind. You suddenly don't care if you miss a few notes – in fact, that ragged style is part of the attraction. Same with *The Shield* – all the camera work is improvised as we shoot, rather than thought out by me far in advance. It's very immediate, very instinctive, very "in the moment." No time for second-guessing or doing careful math, just go go go, shoot shoot shoot! It's nerve-wracking to work that way at first, but I got into it very quickly and loved it. My intention is to adopt this style for *The Mist*. I can always go back to conducting Beethoven later, but *The Mist* will be jazz, stylistically different than any movie I've done.

Probably the smartest move I've made is to hire the team I worked with on *The Shield* to come do *The Mist* with me: the cinematographer, both camera operators, the editor, and the script supervisor. Their skills are very honed in this style after five years of working on that TV show, believe me. They're going to save my ass and make this schedule possible.

Lilja: I suspect that the cast has been selected since shooting starts soon. It's already known that Thomas Jane is in it but can you reveal any other names?

Frank Darabont: Let's see … well, Laurie Holden, who was my leading lady in *The Majestic* and recently played the motorcycle cop in *Silent Hill*. She's probably best known to fans as Marita Covarrubias from *X-Files*. Gorgeous and incredibly talented. Very excited to be working with her again. Also Andre Braugher – a hugely talented man, I've been a fan of his since *Glory*. Frances

Sternhagen, who is a legend, will play Irene … folks may remember her from *Starting Over*, *Outland*, and *Misery*. Alexa Davalos … wow, a remarkable young lady, a stunning new talent. Let me be the first to predict she's going to have an amazing career … remember, you heard it here first. Sam Witwer, a terrific young actor who played Crashdown on *Battlestar Galactica*. Plus a few of my stalwarts that I love working with again and again: Bill Sadler (Heywood in *The Shawshank Redemption* and the father of the two dead girls in *The Green Mile*), Jeff DeMunn (who's been in every movie I've made starting with *The Shawshank Redemption*) … and, hey, I just cast Brian Libby! The real hardcore fans will recognize him as The Prisoner from my Stephen King short, *The Woman in the Room* … plus he was Floyd in *The Shawshank Redemption.* It'll be great to work with him again.

Lilja: Some time ago there *was* a rumor that Michael J. Fox was going to star in it, was there any truth in that?

Frank Darabont: I remember that rumor! That was a persistent one! No, I've actually never met Michael J. Fox, nor had I ever gotten any indication of interest from him. But I am a fan. I was watching *Back to the Future* just last night … it's been all over satellite TV the last few weeks … love that movie, and love him. I'm very sorry he's dealing with the severe health issues he's been facing. He's very courageous. Nobody deserves that … except maybe the assholes in power in this country who are blocking stem cell research at every turn. Those preposterous, uncompassionate turds. God, if you're listening: let *them* get sick, we'll see how fast the arguments go away and the funding happens.

Lilja: The next one is *The Long Walk.* I just heard that you have optioned the film rights for it. How do you plan on realizing it? Some might say that it's just a bunch of kids walking and impossible to turn into a movie...

Frank Darabont: It is just a bunch of kids walking. And talking. And getting shot. That's why I love it. It's a very intense ensemble character piece, another one of those "people in a contained pressure-cooker situation" stories that Steve does so well and seems to specialize in. To me, it's an existential metaphor for our mindless obsession with war – kids being sent off to die for no reason other than "just because." I don't think it's a coincidence that King wrote it in the shadow of Vietnam, though we've never really discussed that part of it, that's just my interpretation. It's a remarkable and pointed piece of fiction, especially considering he was basically a kid when he wrote it. In fact, is it true he started writing it in high school? I suppose I'll ask him, I've always wanted to know. Anyway, chances are *The Long Walk* is more of an art house film than what we'd consider a mainstream Hollywood movie. When I do make it, I'm sure the budget will be even lower than on *The Mist* … a *lot* lower.

Lilja: How far away is *The Long Walk*?

Frank Darabont: Hard to say at this point. I'll get there eventually. Just like I finally got there with *The Mist.*

Lilja: In the book *Creepshow – The Illustrated Stephen King Movie Guide,* author Stephen Jones said that you *were* (the book was released in 2001) planning an official adaptation of King's story *The Monkey*, probably for cable TV. Is there any truth to that and if so, what's happening to it?

Frank Darabont: The same answer as with *The Long Walk. The Monkey* is a story I've always loved, but I have no idea what its commercial viability might be these days as a theatrical feature. It's gentle and old-fashioned Steve King storytelling, not *Saw 2* or *The Grudge*. So maybe doing it as a cable film would be the best option available. I don't know, we'll see, maybe I'll be surprised. But I will get to it one day.

Lilja: Am I missing any King adaptation? Do you have more of them up your sleeve?

Frank Darabont: Steve and I have kicked the idea around of doing *The Dark Tower* some day. Man, I love those books – they're glorious, Steve's magnum opus. But to be honest, it's merely been idle talk. I've told him the thought of adapting that saga makes me break out in a cold sweat, curl into a ball, and weep. It's just so metaphysical and trippy, so much of it is almost impossible stuff to visualize on screen. Not to mention it's just staggeringly huge and massive! I don't think I'd even know where to begin! Hey, you thought *The Green Mile* was long? You ain't seen nothin' yet! I'm afraid *The Dark Tower* might make the expanded Lord of the Rings trilogy look like a short subject. As long-winded as I am, I'm probably better off sticking to Stephen King's short stories and novellas.

Lilja: What else are you working on? I read that you were involved in the fourth Indiana Jones … How does it feel to work on something like that and then find out that they aren't going to use your script?

Frank Darabont: Pretty awful. It was a wasted year or more of my life, and I have only so many years to devote. I worked very closely with Steven Spielberg, applied all my passion and skill, and gave him a script that he loved. He was ready to shoot it that very year – 2003, I think? Maybe 2004? Well, no matter. The point is, Steven was ecstatic. We both were. It was going to be his next film. He told me it was the best script he'd read since *Raiders of the Lost Ark*. That's a quote, and I'll always treasure it. As a screenwriter, you dream of making a guy like Steven Spielberg happy and excited. Then George Lucas read it, didn't like it, and threw ice water on the whole thing. The project went down in flames. Steven and I looked like accident victims the day we got that call. I certainly don't blame Steven for it. He wasn't in a position to overrule George, and wouldn't have overruled him even if he could. He and George have been close friends for a long time, and they've had an agreement for years that no Indiana Jones film will ever get made unless they both completely agreed on the script. It was just such an awful surprise, after all my hopes and effort. I really felt I'd nailed it, and so did Steven.

Yes, as you can imagine, I would rank that very high on my list of professional disappointments. More than that, it was emotionally devastating. For somebody who, as a young man, was inspired to want to be a filmmaker by Steven and George, by movies like *THX-1138* and *Star Wars* and *Raiders of the Lost Ark*, it was the ultimate kick in the nuts. In fact, it's the main reason I quit my career as a "writer-for-hire" (writing for other people for a living). It's not the only reason, but certainly a main reason. I swore never to go through that again. From now on, my intention is to write only for myself on projects that I produce or direct.

You know, I am trying to turn it into something positive. When life hands you a blow like that, I think you should move on as well as you can, or you risk becoming an embittered shithead. I'd rather do the former and not the latter. The experience did get me to refocus my energies on my directing career, which for me always came second to writing. Now it comes first. So maybe it was a blessing in disguise. I don't know … we'll see how it goes with *The Mist* and whatever comes after. If I direct some hits, I'll look like a winner. If I direct some flops, I may eat my words and beg my agents to find me a job rewriting somebody's next movie.

Lilja: How about more books? You have already written *Walpuski's Typewriter* which is a very good book and you have also done a story in *Hellboy: Odder Jobs*. Is writing something you want to continue with?

Frank Darabont: Yes, as we just discussed. Writing is a vital part of what I do … it's part of who I am, really. I can't imagine not being chained to this computer. I'm not sure I'd know what to do with myself. I've spent twenty years here professionally. I'll certainly keep screenwriting, though hopefully not "for hire," assuming the directing goes well. And, yes, I have a novel or two I'd like to try my hand at.

Lilja: In an interview that I did with Stephen King he said you wanted to do a limited edition of *The Mist* (as a book). Can you tell me what you want to do?

Frank Darabont: Well, I'd love to reprint Steve's story in a gorgeous but unpretentious small edition. Even though he's not fond of limiteds, he's thinking it over right now. The last time I heard from him, he said to me, "Frank, I might agree to this, but only if *you* agree to also include your screenplay adaptation, plus some of the pre-production monster art you've been doing." My reply was, "Gee, Steve, twist my arm." My name on the spine of a book alongside Stephen King's? Are you kidding me? Hell, yes! I'm there!

Lilja: In the same interview Stephen King says he isn't that found of limited editions. What is your comment on that?

Frank Darabont: When I read your interview with Stephen King (wonderful interview, congratulations), I had to laugh when I read his comments about limited edition books. I laughed because he and I have had this debate many times. It is a loving debate, as only friends can have. After I read the interview, I sent him an email that said: "Steve, contrary to your notion that people who buy limiteds never read them, I've read every single one of mine, some of them more than once. I had the gigantic *'Salem's Lot* limited from Centipede Press, all twenty pounds of it, resting on my stomach for three nights in a row as I lay in bed. Not only did I enjoy every word of it, but it also strengthened my stomach muscles. And last year I re-read that gorgeous The Stand limited edition published some 15 years ago that looked like the Bible and came in a wooden box. (That *The Stand* limited was actually a gift to me from Steve, which was incredibly generous of him!)

I went on to tell him: "I agree it's absurd to put a book on a shelf and never touch it, as if it were some holy relic instead of a book. That's like being afraid to open a bottle of wine because it's too expensive and rare, or afraid to drive a classic car for the same reason. Wine is meant to be drunk, books are meant to be read, classic cars are meant to be driven -- and I do all three!" (He responded by suggesting that I refrain from doing all three at the same time.)

As I've told Steve in the past, I really feel that presenting a beloved book as a limited edition is a way to honor that literary work and the author responsible for it. The people who create these limiteds do so because they love the book; it shows in the care and quality and effort they put into creating them. I feel it's a huge compliment to the book and its author. I became email friends with Jared Walters (who runs Centipede Press) because I was so knocked out by that awesome huge *'Salem's Lot* he published. So I got in touch to compliment him on it; I sent him a fan letter. And it was very clear to me as we emailed back and forth that he published that limited for one very compelling reason: Jared read *'Salem's Lot* when he was younger, and it changed his life. He loves that book so much that he wanted to honor it, make something special of it, like putting a painting in a perfect frame and hanging it on a wall with just the right lighting. (Jared still hopes to do *The Shining* some day as a limited, and I hope that Steve will eventually allow him. *The Shining* is the very first Stephen King book I ever read, so it's very special to me; it's the book that turned me on to King and led me to be a lifelong fan. It stands as one of Steve's all-time best works, and my personal favorite.)

As for people who buy these books, like me, they do so for the same reason: we love the book. I certainly wouldn't buy a limited of a book I didn't care for just as an investment, or some other silly reason – but for a book I love, how wonderful to have a special edition of it! I've told Steve that as long as the books are also available in low-cost trade editions ("books for the people," as Steve admirably calls them), then what harm is there in doing a small number of special editions for loony, hardcore book lovers like me? It is the difference between buying a gorgeous custom-made chair lovingly handmade by an artisan who withholds no effort in crafting it, and buying a cheap mass-produced chair at IKEA. You can sit on both, they serve the same function, but the aesthetic of the hand-crafted chair makes it a piece of art in itself.

Here's another analogy I've given Steve. You can go see a flawless 65 mm print of Lawrence of Arabia in a beautiful theater with great projection and sound, or you can watch it on a crappy videotape at home. You're seeing the same movie, all the words are there, but the experience is vastly different. The same thing holds true for a book. You can read something on acid-free paper with a hand-sewn binding that your great-grandchildren can read because the book will last for centuries, or you can pick up a paperback that'll turn yellow and fall apart after a few readings.

When I have reverence for a literary work (as I obviously do for King's oeuvre), I love the sense of event and ritual involved in reading a special edition. Opening the box or pulling it from the slipcase … the smell of the binding, the quality of the paper … it's an experience that says: "this book is special to me." It's like seeing that flawless print of Lawrence of Arabia in a theater: by indulging ourselves in the best presentation of that experience, we not only heighten our enjoyment of it, but we also honor the artist who spent years developing his talent and has put so much effort into creating this piece of art that we love. To put it another way, there's just simply a big difference between seeing Monet's Waterlillies reproduced in a book, and seeing the actual canvasses hanging on the wall at the Monet Museum.

Anyway, that's my side of the debate. I love Steve and respect his opinions enormously, but I'm sure our debate will continue and we'll never see totally eye-to-eye on this. Steve always responds to my impassioned perspective by making gagging sounds and yelling: "Books for the people!" I respond to him: "Thank you, Karl Marx, but I want my fucking limiteds. As long as the people aren't starving, I occasionally want filet mignon and a bottle of Mouton Rothschild." It's a pretty funny debate, because Steve and I are politically identical. We're both liberal democrats who believe in compassion and fairness, that everybody in our society should be cared for. But when it comes to limiteds, I'm more like Marie Antoinette: "Let them read paperbacks."

Lilja: I wish you the best of luck with all your upcoming projects and once again, thanks for agreeing to do this interview and please feel free to stop by the site any time!

As you just read, Frank had many Stephen King films planned – *The Long Walk*, *The Monkey*, even *The Dark Tower* were on his radar. Today we know that none of these films were made, or at least not with Frank Darabont as director. But for quite a while the plan was for him to make them all, and I believe that he would have made an excellent job of them.

The next time I talked to Frank was eleven months later, on January 7, 2008, and this time we go deep into *The Mist*. Primarily we discuss the film's ending, which divided film watchers all over the world into two camps: those who find it brilliant, and those who hate it.

Lilja: Hi Frank. It's nice to talk to you again. Last time we talked you where about to shoot *The Mist,* and now it's done and has had its premiere. Are you happy with the result?

Frank Darabont: Delighted. It was deeply satisfying to put this story I've loved for so long on film. The result is the story I always saw in my head when reading the book – and I'm very happy to say that Stephen King loves the movie. That's our best endorsement, as well as my greatest personal satisfaction, the fact that it pleases him.

Also very satisfying for me was the opportunity to try a completely different stylistic approach from anything I'd ever done before as a director, which was very exhilarating and liberating for me. It was a blast, tremendously fun in that regard, and a great learning experience.

Mostly I'm very happy that we accomplished what we set out to do, which was to make a movie on a low budget and a very tight schedule – for the record, it was 17 million dollars and a 37 day shoot. That's not much money these days when major studios are regularly making genre films in the 100 to 200 million dollar budget range. Our goal was to make an ambitious movie with limited resources, very much in the spirit of the grainy low-budget genre films I grew up watching and loving.

Lilja: Personally I really liked *The Mist*. In fact I think it's the best adaptation of a King story to date. What reaction have you gotten on the film? Does everybody like it as much as I do?

Frank Darabont: Thanks, I'm so glad you like it!

Overall, reactions have been very gratifying. A lot of people love it and have blessed us with lavish praise … one critic said it's the best movie of the year and one of the best horror movies ever. I don't know if that's true – time is the only real judge of these things

– but I appreciate the opinion. The people who have embraced the movie love it for the raw quality, the intensity, and the uncompromising ending.

Of course there are some people who hate it too, and I think for those very same reasons. It's real and harsh in a way they don't expect. I think they went in expecting a "popcorn" monster movie with some thrills and a typical ending – a date-night movie, basically – but that's not what they got. They got a bleak, nasty movie that kicked them in the stomach and said some deeply negative things about humanity they weren't prepared to hear. That's not the sort of thing they expect from "just a horror movie," so it pisses them off.

That's okay, you're allowed to hate my movie as much as you're allowed to love it. I always say there's never been a movie that was loved by everybody. (I can read you a few scathingly bad reviews I got for Shawshank when it first came out.) But with *The Mist*, I set out to make a *horror* movie, which by my definition is intended to horrify and disturb you. If the movie did that, I succeeded. Some people love those sensations and admire the result. Some people don't; they'd rather go through the motions of a scary movie but not get kicked in the stomach. They prefer horror that doesn't get too real, and *The Mist* got too real for some people, especially at the end. And that's fair too. Like I said, there's never been a movie that pleases everybody.

What I love is that the film provokes strong reactions either way, but nobody's walking out *unaffected* by it. And that delights me, because I don't want to make a movie that leaves you unaffected, which is the worst way a film can fail … especially a horror film. The films I've loved most in the genre didn't pull their punches, they wanted to fuck with my head. Mind you I'm not comparing my movie with anybody else's or claiming similar greatness – that would be arrogant and idiotic of me – but *Night of the Living Dead* leaps to mind. Man, do I love that film. What a subversive piece of filmmaking that was in its day, and it certainly didn't let us off the hook with warm platitudes or a misplaced happy ending. It kicked us in the stomach instead. So did Carpenter's *The Thing*, another admirably disturbing and subversive film. And Cronenberg's *The Fly*, another masterpiece. Again, I'm not comparing, I'm just bringing these movies up because they've always been genre inspirations for me, iconic high points that took their shit seriously and said something about the human condition. They were made for adults, not the teen date crowd. They did what horror *should* do, I think … take chances, say something, risk pissing you off. *The Thing* certainly pissed a lot of people off when it was originally released in 1982, though I thought it was a classic the moment I saw it.

Lilja: And what an ending! I just loved it. I still have goosebumps from seeing it. I must admit that it's even better than the one King wrote. Did you have to fight to get everyone to agree on having such a dark and sad ending?

Frank Darabont: You can't have an ending as downbeat as this without many people questioning it along the way. Especially on the business end. It certainly scared off a lot of financiers who were otherwise prepared to fund the film. I had a meeting with one producer, very well known, a guy with his own mini-studio. He was prepared to make the movie for 30 million dollars and offered to write me the check before I even left the room. But he insisted I had to change the ending.

It was a tempting offer, but also one of those "do I sell out or not" moments in life. I asked him what he thought the ending should be. He had no idea, all he knew was that he wanted it to be any ending but this one. I told him I had no idea either, that this was the only ending that made sense to me … and I'd been thinking about it for twenty years! So we shook hands and parted ways.

I suppose for the sake of the money, I could have come up with some other ending. But the truth is, I didn't want to sell out. I never have before, and saw no reason to start now. I think it would have been lame to tack on a conclusion that let the main character and the audience off the hook. What would that even be? Suddenly the mist parts and the National Guard is handing them coffee and doughnuts and putting blankets on their shoulders? How obvious and not real. It makes me cringe.

So I ended up making the movie for Bob Weinstein, the only guy with the balls to say, "Hey, I love this, let's make this movie." Of course I had to make the movie for almost half the money the other guy had offered me – 17 million instead of 30. That involved all the typical things: I didn't take a directing salary upfront, everybody was working for reduced fees, we had to very strictly control the spending, etc. But at least I got to make the movie my way. I'm sure some people will think I'm a moron for walking away from all that dough and others will admire my integrity – and, you know, both opinions are fair. But it's not as if I had a choice, really. I have to make the movie I see in my head. I can't render somebody else's creative vision, I can only render my own, for better or worse. It's not even ego – the path I have to follow is the one that makes sense to me, otherwise I'd have no idea what the hell I'm doing.

Lilja: How did you get to think of such a grim ending? I can't even imagine how David feels when he sees the military arriving.

Frank Darabont: It's funny … most people assume I came up with that ending entirely on my own. Even Stephen King thought so. And I haven't yet gone on record to dispute that notion, but I will do so now – a Lilja's Library exclusive! You heard it here first!

Here's the truth: the idea for that ending is right out of Stephen King's book, and I told him so when we were in New York together doing the press junket for the movie. He asked me where I'd gotten the idea. I said, "Steve, I got it from you! Look at this line in your story, here in the last chapter … we're hearing David's thoughts near the end, and it says: 'There are three bullets in the gun, there are four of us in the car. If worse comes to worse, I'll figure a way out for myself.'" (I'm paraphrasing that line right now, but that's essentially what it says.) Steve got this great look on his face when I told him this, because I think he'd forgotten that he ever wrote it.

So all I did was take King's darkest thought and follow it to its most logical and horrible conclusion. The idea for the movie's ending is right there in the original text, I didn't just come up with an idea out of the blue and tack it onto Steve's story. I did what I always do when adapting King or any other author – look for clues in the story that give me insight into the author's thinking and that I can make dramatic use of. I did the same thing quite a bit when adapting *Shawshank* and *Green Mile*.

Lilja: And to make it even worse we get to see the lady that left the store to go home to her children standing among the rescued. Talk about a slap in the face for the others.

Frank Darabont: I think that was a brilliant touch, one of my favorite things in the movie, but I won't take credit for it. Here's how it came about:

When shooting on location (we were in Louisiana), you try to cast the smaller roles with actors who live in that region of the country, especially if your budget is small. The less money you have, the less you can afford to fly actors back and forth from Los Angeles all the time, so it makes financial sense to do as much local casting as possible. The woman I hired to play that role, Melissa McBride, was one of those local actors … she lives in Dallas, I think. She's terrific – I knew from watching her audition tape that she'd be wonderful in the role. Well, the day she played her big scene in the market, she just blew everybody away. The cast, the crew, the extras

– everybody was spellbound by what she was doing. Even our most seasoned actors on the set were trading glances and coming up to me between takes saying, "Wow, where'd you find this woman? She's amazing." When she finished her last take, the entire store burst into applause. It was a wonderful and spontaneous reaction.

About a week later, after Melissa had finished work on the production and gone home, Jeff DeMunn (who plays Dan Miller in the movie) came up to me. Jeff's a sensational actor and one of the dearest men I've ever known. I hope never to make a movie without him, that's how much I love him as a friend and colleague. Anyway, he came up to me and said, "Wow, Melissa McBride sure was great the other day, wasn't she? That character really got under my skin because of how good she was, I can't stop thinking about it." Of course I agreed with everything he was saying. So he took this long pause and said, "Do you think it would be cool if that character was one of the refugees at the end of the movie? Maybe catch a glimpse of her riding past with her kids?"

Awesome idea. And it was Jeff's, based entirely on the excellence of Melissa's work. It shows you the regard actors can have for one another. We called Melissa and invited her back for an additional day of filming. Thank you, Jeff.

Lilja: I just couldn't believe what I saw. And even if it sounds harsh I really like that we didn't get that typical Hollywood ending where all turns out for the best.

Frank Darabont: Thanks, me too. Here's my favorite anecdote about the ending. We did a test screening of the film in Burbank. Two guys came up to me afterward with tears in their eyes and said, "Frank, we love this movie, but we beg you to change the ending, it's too much!" After they were gone, two different guys came up, also with tears in their eyes, and said, "Frank, we love this movie, we beg you not to change the ending, it's perfect!"

As I said, it polarizes audiences. I always figured it would. That's why I was willing to make the movie so cheaply—I always recognized we were taking a risk, but I also knew if we made it cheaply enough the movie would still earn a profit. As you can imagine, I'm very grateful to Bob Weinstein for taking that risk with me.

Lilja: I was also happy to see how good all the actors where. Even though The Mist is a horror movie it's very character driven and really shows how people can act under stress. You must be very proud of them?

Frank Darabont: I'm in awe of my cast. And my crew – let's not exclude them, because they are just as important. Everybody went above and beyond the call of duty and I couldn't have done it without each of them committing as passionately and working as hard as they did. I'm extremely grateful to them all.

But back to the cast – yes, I'm deeply proud. They excelled, especially considering how fast we were shooting. I say it's the best work Thomas Jane has ever done, period. Of all his roles so far, this is the one that offered him the most depth as a character. And he made the most of that. He showed up hungry to delve into the emotional layers of the role, not just rely on being the "action hero." That guy's a real actor, and he just nailed it. He's really surprised people because he's so damn good.

Laurie Holden, I think it's her best work too – this allowed her to play raw and real in a way her earlier roles haven't, and I include my own film *The Majestic* in that. She was brilliant in that film, but *Majestic* required that she play an idealized "girl next door" perfection. Her character was filtered through a strong romantic perception of a time and place – that's what the role demanded because it was a sweet period piece with a slightly unreal Frank Capra quality, more idealized than real life. And Laurie did it beautifully. But in *The Mist*, she gets to play real. A real person you'd meet in line at the market. Raw and earthbound, ballsy, nothing stylized. And she rocks.

Marcia Gay Harden, Andre Braugher ... they rock too. I found out when we were shooting that they've been friends forever. As actors they're both forces of nature. Their skills are so sharply honed that being on the set and watching them play their scenes is electrifying. A thrill. All a director has to do is point the camera at them and you're mining gold. Absolute professionals. I'm so happy and grateful that they graced our movie with their presence. They brought a texture to the film that is irreplaceable.

I'll say that for the rest of the cast as well. There's a reason I love working with guys like Jeff DeMunn and Bill Sadler again and again – they're awesome, a pleasure, total pros. Most of all, they make every film they're in more memorable by their presence.

Crap! Now I'm in trouble because I've mentioned some actors by name, so now I have to mention them all – but I have a big cast! I do want to acknowledge them all though, because they richly deserve it, but I'll go quickly:

Frances Sternhagen. I've been a huge fan of hers since the movie *Starting Over*. I was so honored to work with her at last. Talk about a pro, a delight. And apparently tireless! All that running she did at her age, and never a word of complaint.

Alexa Davalos. An amazing young talent. Check out Robert Benton's film *Feast of Love*, or Ed Zwick's next movie (sorry, I forget the title, but it's his next one coming up [that film was *Defiance*, 2008]). Keep your eye on Alexa, folks, because she's going to be a significant actress with a major career. I'm not kidding. And remember you heard it here first.

Sam Witwer. He nailed his audition for *The Mist* so perfectly that I never even looked at another actor for the role, I just hired him immediately. He's exceptional. I love his enthusiasm. He's a science-fiction/horror geek like me. Fans will know him from his exemplary work on *Battlestar Galactica* and *Dexter*.

Nathan Gamble. Wow, what a wonderful kid. Everybody fell in love with him—*and* his family, who are the nicest people ever. I've never seen a 9 year-old with such a mature grasp of what he's doing. He's got serious talent. My favorite scene in the movie is when he's sobbing and begging Tom not to go to the pharmacy – the actors are superb there, but keep in mind that Nathan's only nine years old! And he's playing it with as much power and conviction as the adults. No tricks or makeup involved, either – all those tears, everything was just purely Nathan's performance. I remember when we shot that, people were gathered around the monitors just blown away by what he was doing.

I haven't yet mentioned Toby Jones because I peeked ahead and saw your next question. But before we move on to him, let me also acknowledge Rob Treveiler (Bud), David Jensen (Myron), and Chris Owen (Norm) – superb character actors in the Jeff DeMunn and Bill Sadler tradition. They too brought something special to the movie and I loved working with them. Oh, and Jack Hurst, too! The burned guy. I love all my actors and could rave about them all day. Even the extras did an amazing job.

Lilja: Even though everyone is very good I'm most impressed by the casting of Toby Jones as Ollie. He is perfect. Was he your first choice?

Frank Darabont: Toby was *not* my first choice, but that's only because I wasn't yet aware of him. He's from England and wasn't well known here at that time (but that's changing). And I hadn't yet seen his work in *Infamous* or *Painted Veil* when we started casting last year. But my casting director, Deb Aquila, told me to watch those films immediately because she was crazy for Toby and was convinced he should play Ollie. I watched both films and loved them, *Painted Veil* especially. Toby just shines in both. Of course now he'd *always* be my first choice. He's an extraordinary actor. His Ollie is perfection.

By the way, are you aware Toby's father is the great British character actor Freddie Jones? Look him up on IMDB, he'll blow your mind – he played Mr. Bytes in *The Elephant Man*, among hundreds of other roles. When I first met Toby and realized who his dad is, I totally geeked out. Toby was surprised I knew who his dad is and that I'm such a big fan.

Lilja: Now I guess we just have to wait for the Oscar nominations to see how many *The Mist* gets? Both *The Shawshank Redemption* and *The Green Mile* have been nominated and even though it's harder for a horror movie to be nominated there are a lot of actors in *The Mist* that ought to be.

Frank Darabont: I appreciate your kind thought, but there's no way we'll get any nominations. A low-budget horror movie like ours isn't even on the Oscar radar screen. I do agree my actors would be deserving of recognition for the work they've done – perhaps they'd get that recognition if they'd been in another kind of movie – but not this one.

Lilja: Last time we spoke you mentioned that you might do a limited book version of *The Mist*. Is that still the plan?

Frank Darabont: Yes. I'm working on it now and hoping to have it out in time for the DVD release. That would be excellent timing.

Lilja: What can you tell me about *The Mist* DVD? What can we expect to find on it except the movie?

Frank Darabont: We're discussing those now, but no decisions have been made yet.

Lilja: How about a script book of *The Mist*. Like the ones we got for *The Shawshank Redemption* and *The Green Mile*? Any plans for such a book?

Frank Darabont: Here's another Lilja exclusive: The limited will include both Stephen King's original story *and* my screenplay. That's not the way I originally planned it – I always figured I would just present Steve's story by itself. But suddenly Steve had the idea to include my screenplay too. In fact, he insisted on it – he said he'd only agree to do the book if we included both. He didn't have to try very hard to convince me. I told him I'd be very honored to be in the same book with him.

Lilja: Your next Stephen King movie is *The Long Walk*, right? Where are you with that one now? Is a script written?

Frank Darabont: There isn't a script yet. I plan to write it this year.

Lilja: I guess that script will demand a lot if you're going to succeed in making it into a feature film. *The Long Walk* is one of my favorite books but you must admit that it's not the first book you're thinking of when you think of a Stephen King book turned into a movie. What got you hooked on that particular book and aren't you worried that it's not doable as a movie?

Frank Darabont: What makes *The Long Walk* a great story is how stripped-down and spare it is. Not much plot – just kids walking, talking, and dying. It's a very existential work, Stephen King meets Eugene Ionesco. And that's what I love about it. It's small and fascinating and weird, and I think the movie should be too. It's more of an art house movie the way Steve wrote it. I don't want to reinvent it or blow it out of proportion to justify it as a big commercial film, which is how they screwed up *The Running Man*. I'm not sure it's even possible with material like *The Long Walk*. Of course doing it faithfully means I'd have to do it cheaply – far more cheaply than *The Mist* – but at least I can stay true to what Steve wrote. Perhaps as a cool little film for HBO or Showtime?

Lilja: Last time you also mentioned *The Monkey*? Any news on that one?

Frank Darabont: I'm hoping to write that script this year too. We'll see how it turns out. It might make a good theatrical feature. We'll see.

Lilja: Any other King/Darabont collaborations that you can talk about?

Frank Darabont: We're going to have a baby through in-vitro fertilization. No, that's not true. I'm just messing around. I should know better, because that's how rumors get started.

Lilja: What else are you up to? I guess you might be taking a well-deserved break now that *The Mist* is done.

Frank Darabont: Yes, I need it. I've never made a movie this quickly. We started prepping the film in January and we finished everything at the end of October – ten months of production from start to finish. (Plus I did a few months prior to that casting actors with Deb and designing monsters with Nicotero, so maybe twelve months for me in all?) I'm glad I did it, I'm glad I proved I *could* do it, but I don't want to do it that way often. It kills you, it's intense and exhausting. What I learned making *The Mist* is that it's just as hard making a 17 million dollar movie as it is making a 67 million dollar film like Green Mile. But with a bigger budget, you at least have the additional advantage of time.

Lilja: When can we expect a new book from you? I enjoyed *Walpuski's Typewriter* a lot and would really like another book.

Frank Darabont: Thanks! I remember that great review you wrote, it really made my day. Did you also happen to see my short story in the book *Odder Jobs*, the Hellboy anthology edited by Chris Golden? My story's sort of a Twilight Zone-style western called "Brotherhood of the Gun". I'm proud of that little story, it was tremendously satisfying and fun to do.

I am working on a few book or short story projects like those right now, but nothing worth mentioning because I don't know if they'll ever be finished. Writing prose fiction is a very part-time thing for me, something I do just for enjoyment on the rare occasion that I have spare time from my real job. It's great writing just for the pleasure of it, with no financial or career objectives attached, or the pressure of a film production involved. But of course those pressures tend to get things done. When you're writing solely for pleasure, things have a way of never getting completed.

Lilja: OK, thanks for taking the time to talk to me. I enjoyed it!

My next conversation with Frank occurred only two months after the second one, and this time is focused on the DVD release of *The Mist*, particularly on the black-and-white version of the film which is included. The interview was made on March 25, 2008, and I have edited it slightly since some of the subjects touched on are basically the same as in the earlier interviews.

Lilja: Hello Frank! I hope everything is well with you.

Frank Darabont: Everything is great, thanks for asking.

Lilja: So, you know I'm a big fan of *The Mist*.

Frank Darabont: Yeah, thank you very much.

Lilja: And I'm very happy to see that it's out on DVD soon. I watched it this weekend. And I have to say … well I actually watched the black and white version …

Frank Darabont: Oh, you did, what did you think? Be honest, which one do you like better?

Lilja: I actually liked the black and white best.

Frank Darabont: Ah, excellent

Lilja: It makes the movie a bit darker and more chilling.

Frank Darabont: Yes, oh good, I'm glad.

Lilja: What kind of reactions have you gotten on the movie?

Frank Darabont: The DVD is coming out here on the 25th but for some reason a lot of people have seen it already. I handed it out to some friends of mine, like Tarantino and guys like that and I think the reaction to the black and white is bigger than I realized that it was going to be. Everyone is kind of silly excited about it. And the people who have seen it in black and white have gotten back to me and their reaction is fantastic. It just tells me it was a pretty good idea to do it that way … for people who enjoy that kind of approach.

Lilja: Did you actually plan to release it in black and white when you shot it or was it just a bonus that the studio was willing to release it on the DVD?

Frank Darabont: Well, I was always … even when we were shooting, even before we were shooting I knew I was going to shoot it in color, obviously, but I was hoping that a black and white conversion might be good for the movie. You can never really tell until you do it. I was very pleasantly surprised at how well it did adapt, retimed as a black and white film. It was the Coen brothers who gave me the idea really because they shot *The Man Who Wasn't There* in color but they released it as a black and white film. They had retimed it for a black and white release and I thought that that looked so good; I thought the same thing might apply to my film. But I think this is the first time anyone has released both versions, both the color and black and white version.

Lilja: I hope you're setting a trend because it was quite a different experience to see it in black and white. It was also very nice to have both on the DVD.

Frank Darabont: Yeah, it's a totally different viewing experience, I think, and maybe it'll be a trend, who knows? We'll see how this goes over but my fellow film makers are very intrigued by it.

Lilja: But I also think it has to be a very special type of movie that make do the transition from color to black and white and still be as good or even better.

Frank Darabont: Yeah, it totally depends on the movie, I think. It totally depends on the material and the photography.

Lilja: When you read reactions to the movie it seems that most fans really like the movie, but it also seems like the ending has divided the fans into two camps. One that really loves it and one that doesn't like it at all.

Frank Darabont: That hates it. Let's use the proper word. [laugh] You know, I always knew that it was going to be a very divisive and polarizing ending in that way. I know that some people would absolutely love it and that some people wouldn't, but it always felt like the correct ending to me.

Lilja: Yes, I agree.

Frank Darabont: And there is a part of me that takes great pleasure in the fact that it does divide the audience in that way because it indicates that the movie took the right chances.

Lilja: [laughs] I'm very happy that you stuck to the original ending and not a happy Hollywood ending.

Frank Darabont: Thank you, me too. I still don't know what the other ending would be.

Lilja: No, I don't think there is another ending that would actually work. It's like you say in … I think it's in the commentary, that every century needs a movie like *Night of the Living Dead* where everybody dies in the end …

Frank Darabont: Yeah, that's what Stephen King said to me when he read this ending originally. I was very concerned. You know the ending was taking a chance, taking a risk and I wanted to make sure it was in Stephen King's language as well. I wanted to know that I had his approval on something like that and that was his reaction. He said, "I love this ending, I'm sorry I didn't think of it" and "every generation needs a movie like this where nothing turns out well". This is a horror movie. It should horrify and disturb the audience.

Lilja: When I saw the movie I actually think it benefitted from being a low budget movie and done very quickly, is that your feeling too now that it's done?

Frank Darabont: Definitely my feeling and it was even my feeling when we were shooting it because there were so much wonderful ragged energy going into the filming even as we were shooting it and I thought "this is wonderful, that we've done it on this basis" and the truth is that I wanted to embrace the aesthetic of the low budget horror movie so we embraced it on a very practical level which is "OK, well then, let's do it really low budget". [laugh] And we have. Some of my favorite movies in the genre were made that way and it felt like an honest way to do it.

Lilja: But it's not the usual way for you to make your movies?

Frank Darabont: No, completely different, completely different style, completely different approach. It was very exciting for me to do something completely outside my previous knowledge, to get me out of my comfort zone of what I do and what I know how to do and try something completely different. And part of what allowed that was indeed the low budget because if I had twice the money maybe I would have been a little more careful in how I shot it. As it was I had no time to be careful at all and that I think brought this wonderful energy into this thing. And it was really fun to do it that way I have to say.

Lilja: It was really fun to listen to your commentary, especially where you describe how easily and with quite small means you managed to get the right feeling and the effect that you wanted.

Frank Darabont: We had such a wonderful team in place. Greg Nicotero, Erin Borel and so many other people I've worked with in the past on low budget films. And it's, in a weird way, very liberating to have to come up with clever solutions rather than just throw money at a problem. You have to come up with a clever solution on how to do something and when you have a team like that it's marvelous, because we're all working towards the same goal.

Lilja: And now that the movie is done, is this something you want to do again with another movie, or is it back to your normal way of making movies?

Frank Darabont: Well, I don't want do it all the time [laugh] cause it's a tremendous challenge, I'd like to have a little more luxury of time next time, but when I do *The Long Walk* that will be even more low budget than this one was, I'm certain of it.

Lilja: Do you have any plans for *The Long Walk* now? Are you working on it at the moment?

Frank Darabont: It's on one of the burners on the stove, you know. It's not on the front burner at the moment but I imagine it's going to be something that I'll do probably within the next five years. I don't have any immediate plans …

Lilja: It will be very interesting to see that one made into a movie.

Frank Darabont: That one will be very, very faithful to Stephen's story, even more faithful than *The Mist* was. But it doesn't bear a huge budget because it's a very existential strange little story. If you do it faithfully it winds up being a strange little movie so not a blockbuster, just a very interesting film I think.

Lilja: I think that potentially it could be a very good movie if it's done right.

Frank Darabont: Thank you. Well, I think it's one of Steve's best stories; it's so strange and brilliant, isn't it?

Lilja: Yeah, it's amazing to be able to make a story about people who are just walking.

Frank Darabont: Exactly! And what it is, is Stephen King meets Eugene Ionesco and I definitely want the movie to have that same feeling.

Lilja: I did an interview with Stephen King earlier and he mentioned that you wanted him to play a part in *The Mist*.

Frank Darabont: Yes, I did. I wanted him to play the biker. I wanted to really get a performance out of him and really treat him like any other actor in the piece rather than an "Oh, here is the Stephen King cameo", you know. So, I wanted him to grow a big biker beard and when I mixed the film and the sound I'd pitch his voice just a bit lower so you wouldn't necessarily immediately recognize his voice. I wanted to see if I could fool the audience into thinking it was just another actor …

Lilja: It would have been very nice to have seen him in that part.

Frank Darabont: Yeah, I was really looking forward to that, but he didn't have the time to do it, I'm sure he told you…

Lilja: Yeah, but you got a lot of references to him anyway; the books, *The Dark Tower* poster and a lot of other things.

Frank Darabont: Absolutely, and also the good news of not being able to use Steve is that I was able to use Brian Libby who is a very old friend of mine and he is a very good reference to Stephen King because he was in *The Shawshank Redemption* and he was in my short film *The Woman in the Room* years and years ago so it was wonderful to work with Brian again and give him an opportunity on screen again. He's just a terrific presence.

Lilja: Yeah, very nice. Okay, then, thank you very much for doing this interview. I hope we'll talk soon again.

Frank Darabont: Very soon, I so appreciate it.

So far I have not interviewed Frank Darabont again since the above, but I hope to get the chance to talk to him again. He is a gratifying person to interview, always open and willing to talk freely. Let me add that he was also very generous in sending me two fake newspapers used in *The Mist*, as well as signed posters for all of his three feature films based on Stephen King stories.

Afterword

That's it for this time. For starting out as a book which would never get written, this one ended up being considerably longer than its predecessors. How could that happen? Well, there are times when you just have to accept that things turn out as they do.

Now, however, my ideas folder is empty (except for that notion of writing about Stephen King's philanthropy), so this time I actually believe that I've written my last book about Stephen King.

Though come to think of it, I do have that idea about …

Author’s note

As always, I want to thank some persons before we close the book for good. People without whose help I probably wouldn’t have written this book at all, or if I had it would at least have been a lesser work for lack of their input, support and assistance.

Anders Jakobson. There is no other person I have talked as much to about Stephen King. I’m glad he is as interested in the subject as I am. Many thanks for all your excellent ideas!

My test readers – Carina Holm, Malin Karlbrink, Malin Hammarström, Daniel Gustavsson, Markus Widerberg, Lini Forsberg and, again, Anders Jakobson. Thank you for valuable comments, corrections, encouragement, tips and viewpoints.

My Italian publisher, Independent Legions, my Czech publisher, Carcosa, my German publisher Buchheim Verlag, and my American publisher, BearManor Media, who all dared take a chance on this book and contracted it unseen. If you hadn’t, it might never have been written. Thank you.

John Ajvide Lindqvist, whose encouragement and queries about when my next book on King was due meant more than he probably realizes. And thanks for the title!

Last but anything but least, Stephen King. Without you there would most definitely not have been any book.

My thanks to all of you,
Hans-Åke Lilja
Örebro, January 26, 2025

Appendix: Stephen King's book dedications

Book: *Carrie* (Doubleday, 1974)
Dedication: *This is for Tabby, who got me into it – and then bailed me out of it.*
Explanation: Tabby is a nickname for Stephen King's wife Tabitha. *Carrie* was his first published book; King himself had written the beginning of it, found it wanting, and discarded it. Tabitha King picked it out of his wastebasket, convinced him to finish it, and after *Carrie* everything else followed.

Book: *Salem's Lot* (Doubleday, 1975)
Dedication: *For Naomi Rachel King "... promises to keep."*
Explanation: Naomi is Stephen and Tabitha King's daughter. What he has promised her, only Stephen King himself knows ... and of course his daughter.

Book: *The Shining* (Doubleday, 1977)
Dedication: *This is for Joe Hill King, who shines on.*
Explanation: Joe, the oldest son to Stephen and Tabitha King, was born in 1972 and according to those who know him personally has always had a kind of "shine", an openness. Possibly that is what is alluded to here. Or maybe King simply thought it fit in with the book's title (just as he did when he wrote "For Hans-Åke Lilja – keep shining on!" in my book *Shining in the Dark* [Cemetery Dance, 2017]).

Book: *Rage* (as by Richard Bachman, Signet, 1977)
Dedication: *For Susan Artz and WGT.*

Explanation: Susan Artz was one of King's earliest teachers. In manuscript, this novel was called *Getting It On*, and at that time it was dedicated to her alone. WGT stands for William G. Thompson, who was King's editor at Doubleday. Thompson several times tried to persuade Doubleday to publish *Getting It On*, but never succeeded. Finally, it was released as an original paperback and under the pen name "Richard Bachman". Though since King at the time kept his "Bachman" pseudonym secret, it was perhaps a bit risky to dedicate the novel to two persons so close to him.

Book: *The Stand* (Doubleday, 1978)
Dedication: *For my wife Tabitha: This dark chest of wonders*
Explanation: A second dedication to King's wife Tabitha.

Book: *The Long Walk* (as by Richard Bachman, Signet, 1979)
Dedication: *This is for Jim Bishop and Burt Hatlen and Ted Holmes.*
Explanation: All the three men named were teachers at the University of Maine when King studied there, and all three both influenced King and urged him to continue with the novel after reading an early draft. Again, King takes a risk when dedicating a "Richard Bachman" novel to persons who had meant something to King.

Book: *The Dead Zone* (Doubleday, 1978)
Dedication: *THIS IS FOR OWEN I LOVE YOU, OLD BEAR*
Explanation: Now King's and his wife's youngest son gets a dedication, meaning that everyone in the family has had at least one.

Book: *Firestarter* (Doubleday, 1980)
Dedication: *In memory of Shirley Jackson, who never needed to raise her voice.*
The Haunting of Hill House
The Lottery
We Have Always Lived in the Castle
The Sundial.

Explanation: Shirley Jackson (1916–1965) was an author greatly admired by Stephen King. The four book titles listed are tree of her novels and one story collection, all notable for their emphasis on psychological suspense.

Book: *Danse Macabre* (Everest House, 1981)
Dedication: *It's easy enough – perhaps too easy – to memorialize the dead. This book is for sex great writers of the macabre who are still alive.*
Robert Bloch
Jorge Luis Borges
Ray Bradbury
Frank Belknap Long
Donald Wandrei
Manly Wade Wellman. Enter, Stranger, at your own Riske: Here there be Tygers.
Explanation: Danse Macabre was a very personal non-fiction book about horror in fiction and films up until its release; it concentrated on the authors King had appreciated under his own reading in the field.

Book: *Roadwork* (as by Richard Bachman, Signet, 1981)
Dedication: *In memory of Charlotte Littlefield. Proverbs 31:10–28*
Explanation: Charlotte Littlefield was one of Stephen King's teachers at Hampden Academy. The Bible verses referred to describe "A wife of noble character … worth far more than rubies."

Book: Cujo (Viking, 1981)
Dedication: *This is for my brother, David, who held my hand crossing West Broad Street, and who taught me how to make skyhooks out of old coat hangers. The trick was so damned good I just never stopped. I love you, David.*
Explanation: David King was Stephen King's adopted older brother (1945–2021).

Book: *The Dark Tower I: The Gunslinger* (Grant, 1982)
Dedication: *To ED FERMAN who took a chance on these stories, one by one.*
Explanation: Edward "Ed" Ferman was for many years the editor and publisher of *The Magazine of Fantasy and Science Fiction*, where the five stories making up *The Gunslinger* were originally published from 1978 through 1981.

Book: Christine (Viking, 1983)
Dedication: *This is for George Romero and Chris Forrest Romero. And the Burg.*
Explanation: Romero (1940–2017) was the legendary director of almost only horror movies, including the groundbreaking *Night of the Living Dead* (1968) and *Creepshow* (1982), based on five Stephen King stories and with King himself as the main character in one of the stories. Christine ("Chris") Forrest Romero was the director's second wife. Later, the couple worked on filming King's short novel *The Girl Who Loved Tom Gordon*. "The Burg" in this case is a nickname for Pittsburgh, where many of George Romero's films are set.

Book: *Cycle of the Werewolf* (Land of Enchantment, 1983)
Dedication: *In memory of Davis Grubb, and all the voices of Glory*
Explanation: Davis Grubb (1919–1980) was a novelist and short story writer; *The Voices of Glory* was one of his novels, although his most famous was *The Night of the Hunter*, filmed in 1955. King has named him as an author who influenced him.

Book: *Pet Sematary* (Doubleday, 1983)
Dedication: *For Kirby McCauley.*
Explanation: Kirby McCauley (1941–2014) was Stephen King's first literary agent, helped him keep the "Richard Bachman" pen name secret and took out the copyright on all except the first of the Bachman's novels in his own name, and was as well a personal friend of the Kings.

Book: *The Talisman* (with Peter Straub, Viking, 1984)
Dedication: *This book is for*
RUTH KING
ELVENA STRAUB
Ruth King was Stephen King's mother, Elvena Straub was Peter Straub's mother.

Book: *Thinner* (New American Library, 1984)
Dedication: *To my wife, Claudia Inez Bachman*
Explanation: In the made up story of "Richard Bachman", he was married to Claudia and had a son who was never named but who had according to the story fallen through the lid covering the well on the family farm and tragically drowned. Since *Thinner* was the first of the Bachman novels to be published in hardcover, it was for obvious reasons he dedicated it to his wife.

Book: *The Eyes of the Dragon* (Philtrum Press, 1984)
Dedication: *This story is for my great friend BEN STRAUB, and for my daughter NAOMI KING.*
Explanation: Benjamin "Ben" Straub is Peter Straub's son, who also gave his name to one of the characters in the novel, Ben Staad. King wrote the book for his daughter, who has also lent her name to one of the characters in the story, Naomi.

Book: *Skeleton Crew* (Putnam, 1985)
Dedication: *This book is for Arthur and Joyce Greene*
Explanation: Arthur Greene was Stephen King's lawyer, Joyce of course was Arthur's wife.

Book: *It* (Viking, 1986)
Dedication: *This book is gratefully dedicated to my children. My mother and my wife taught me how to be a man. My children taught me how to be free.*
NAOMI RACHEL KING, at fourteen;
JOSEPH HILLSTROM KING, at twelve;

OWEN PHILIP KING, at seven.
Kids, fiction is the truth inside the lie, and the truth of this fiction is simple enough: The magic exists. S.K.
Explanation: No explanation needed for this one.

Book: *The Dark Tower II: The Drawing of the Three* (Grant, 1987)
Dedication: *To Don Grant, who's taken a chance on these novels, one by one.*
Explanation: Donald M. Grant (1927–2009) was the founder of Donald M. Grant, Publisher who released The Dark Tower books. Grant here receives a thank you similar to that King gave Edward Ferman in *The Gunslinger*.

Book: *Misery* (Viking, 1987)
Dedication: *This is for Stephanie and Jim Leonard, who know why. Boy, do they.*
Explanation: Stephanie is Tabitha King's sister and was the editor of *Castle Rock*, a monthly newsletter for Stephen King enthusiasts and readers published from January, 1985, until December, 1989. For a time she was also King's assistant. Jim, Stephanie's husband, took care of the King family's house. Both of them met quite a few King fans in their respective functions.

Book: *The Tommyknockers* (Putnam, 1987)
Dedication: *For Tabitha King "... promises to keep."*
Explanation: Stephen King's wife Tabitha again. *The Tommyknockers* was published in 1987, and the year before King after a family intervention had quit both drinking and drugs. Perhaps the promises quoted have something to do with that.

Book: *The Dark Half* (Viking, 1989)
Dedication: *This book is for Shirley Sonderegger, who helps me mind my business, and for her husband, Peter.*
Explanation: Shirley Sonderegger handled all of King's correspondence with readers during most of the 1980s. She has said

that among the more bizarre parcels she opened was one containing the furs and skeletons of kittens, and another containing a scorpion. She is obviously married to Peter.

Book: *The Stand: The Complete and Uncut edition* (Doubleday. 1990)
Dedication: *FOR TABBY this dark chest of wonders*
Explanation: A slightly changed version of the dedication in the earlier, shorter version of *The Stand.*

Book: *The Dark Tower III: The Waste Lands* (Donald M. Grant, 1991)
Dedication: *This third volume of the tale is gratefully dedicated to my son, OWEN PHILIP KING: Khef, ka, and Ka-tet.*
Explanation: Another dedication to King's youngest son Owen (to whom he had earlier dedicated *The Dead Zone*, 1979). At StephenKing.com there is a glossary explaining the made-up words in "The Dark Tower" series of books, and if you look under "High Speech" you find these explanations for the three words used in the dedication:
Khef = Literally speaking, *khef* means "the sharing of water." It also implies birth, life force, and all that is essential to existence. Khef can only be shared by those whom destiny has welded together for good or ill—in other words, by those who are Ka-tet.
Ka = It signifies life force, consciousness, duty, and destiny.
Ka-tet = *Ka-tet* means "one made from many." *Ka* refers to destiny; *tet* refers to a group of people with the same interests or goals. Ka-tet is the place where men's lives are joined by fate.

Book: *Needful Things* (Viking, 1991)
Dedication: *This is for Chris Lavin, who doesn't have all the answers – just the ones that matter.*
Explanation: King knew Chris Lavin already at the University of Maine where Chris got a Bachelor of Arts in 1971 and then a Master of Library Service in 1973. King also named the character

Christopher Lavin, the first Junction City Librarian in "The Library Policeman", after him. That character also had a degree in Library Science.

Book: *Gerald's Game* (Viking, 1992)
Dedication: *This book is dedicated with love and admiration to six good women:*
Margaret Spruce Morehouse
Catherine Spruce Graves
Stephanie Spruce Leonard
Anne Spruce Labree
Tabitha Spruce King
Marcella Spruce
Explanation: A novel about a strong woman must obviously be dedicated to strong women. Here King lists six women he admires. Tabitha is a given, and the other five women are all Tabitha's sisters.

Book: *Dolores Claiborne* (Viking, 1993)
Dedication: *For my mother, Ruth Pillsbury King*
Explanation: *Dolores Claiborne* and *Gerald's Game* are variations on a theme; since King dedicated the first of them to "strong women" – his wife and her sisters, it feels only reasonable that he dedicates the second to another strong woman, his mother.

Book: *Nightmares & Dreamscapes* (Viking, 1993)
Dedication: *In memory of THOMAS WILLIAMS, 1926–1990:*
Poet, novelist, and
Great American Storyteller.
Explanation: Thomas Williams was a literature teacher and novelist; Stephen King has said that Williams' 1974 novel *The Hair of Harold Roux* has remained one of his favorite books and that he returns to it "again and again".

Book: *Insomnia* (Viking, 1994)
Dedication: *For Tabby ... and for Al Kooper, who knows the playing-field. No fault of mine.*
Explanation: ”Tabby” is, again, King’s wife Tabitha; Al Kooper is a songwriter, musician and record producer. Since he is also a published author he could join the Rock Bottom Remainders, the band of writers to which King belongs, and in 1993 King and the others went on tour and later published a book about it, *Mid-life Confidential: The Rock Bottom Remainders Tour America with Three Chords and an Attitude*; Kooper acted as the band’s musical director. Tabitha took some of the photos in the book.

Book: *Rose Madder* (Viking, 1995)
Dedication: *This book is for Joan Marks.*
Explanation: Joan Marks is a social worker in Portland; she helped Stephen King on his research for parts of this novel.

Book: *Desperation* (Viking, 1996)
Dedication: *For Carter Withey*
Explanation: Carter Withey managed King’s book tour (on motorcycle) for *Insomnia*; they became close friends, and later among other things did a month-long drive around Australia.

Book: *The Regulators* (as by Richard Bachman; Viking, 1996)
Dedication: *Thinking of Jim Thompson and Sam Peckinpah: Legendary shadows.*
Explanation: Jim Thompson (1906–1977) was one of the finest of the ”noir” crime writers, famous not least for his 1952 novel *The Killer Inside Me*; King holds him in high regard. Sam Peckinpah (1925–1984) was an acclaimed director. A few months before his death, he and King had agreed to cooperate on a film called ”The Shotgunners”, to be written by King and directed by Peckinpah. The film was never made, but its outline served as the basis for *The Regulators*.

Book: *The Dark Tower IV: Wizard and Glass* (Grant, 1997)
Dedication: *This book is dedicated to Julie Eugley and Marsha DeFilippo. They answer the mail, and most of the mail for the last couple of years has been around Roland of Gilead – the gunslinger. Basically, Julie and Marsha nagged me back to the word processor. Julie, you nagged the most effectively, so your name comes first.*
Explanation: Six years passed between the third and the fourth book in King's "Dark Tower" series. During that time readers kept writing King to ask when the next book would appear. Most of that mail was handled by his assistants Julie Eugley and Marsha DeFilippo, who by handling disgruntled readers for years, richly deserved their dedication.

Book: *Bag of Bones* (Scribner, 1998)
Dedication: *This is for Naomi. Still.*
Explanation: Another book for Stephen and Tabitha Kings' daughter Naomi.

Book: *The Girl Who Loved Tom Gordon* (Scribner, 1999)
Dedication: *This is for my son Owen, who ended up teaching me a lot more about the game of baseball than I ever taught him.*
Explanation: A book about a girl loving baseball for a King's younger son, who loves baseball.

Book: *Hearts in Atlantis* (Scribner, 1999)
Dedication: *This is for Joseph and Leanora and Ethan: I told you all that to tell you this.*
Explanation: The novel, largely about the America of King's own youth, is dedicated to his son Joe, Joe's then wife (they divorced in 2010) and their first child.

Book: *Dreamcatcher* (Scribner, 2001)
Dedication: This is for Susan Moldow and Nan Graham.
Explanation: Susan Moldow was King's editor at Scribner before becoming president of the Scribner Publishing Group; Nan Graham

was editor-in-chief of Scribner from the early 1990s, later its publisher. They both worked with Stephen King.

Book: *Black House* (with Peter Straub, Random House, 2001)
Dedication: *For David Gernert and Ralph Vicinanza.*
Explanation: Another novel written with Peter Straub. David Gernert was Straub's literary agent, Ralph Vicinanza was King's, until his unexpected early death in 2010.

Book: *Everything's Eventual* (Scribner, 2002)
Dedication: *This is for Shane Leonard*
Explanation: Stephanie Leonard is Stephen King's sister; her husband Shane is consequently King's brother-in-law. He is also a photographer and has taken several of the publicity photos King has used.

Book: From a Buick 8 (Scribner, 2002)
Dedication: *This is for Surendra and Geeta Patel.*
Explanation: Surendra Patel was an accountant and a close friend of Stephen King. Geeta Patel we can assume was his wife, or possibly daughter.

Book: *The Dark Tower V: Wolves of the Calla* (Grant/Scribner, 2003)
Dedication: *This book is for Frank Muller, who hears the voices in my head.*
Explanation: Frank Muller (1951–2008) was a stage and voice actor who read many of Stephen King's audiobook publications. In 2001 he was in a severe motorcycle accident which rendered him unable to do further work.

Book: *The Dark Tower VI: Song of Susannah* (Grant/Scribnet, 2004)
Dedication: *For Tabby, who knew when it was done.*
Again a book dedicated to Tabitha King.

Book: *The Dark Tower VII: The Dark Tower* (Donald M. Grant/ Scribner 2004)
Dedication: *He who speaks without an attentive ear is mute. Therefore, Constant Reader, this final book in the Dark Tower cycle is dedicated to you. Long days and pleasant nights.*
Explanation: This is where Stephen King thanks all the readers who have followed the story of Roland and his friends and enemies, and where he points out that lacking his readers, his words would have had no audience and so found no listeners.

Book: *Faithful* (with Stewart O'Nan, Scribner, 2004)
Dedication: *For Victoria Snelgrove, Red Sox fan*
Explanation: The book is a non-fiction chronicle of the Boston Red Sox baseball team's 2004 season, ending in their triumph. The authors dedicated their book to Victoria Snelgrova, a journalism student who was accidentally killed by a policeman during the unruly clashes in Fenway Park between Red Sox fans and New York Yankees fans after the Boston team beat the Yankees for the American League championship.

Book: *The Colorado Kid* (Hard Case, 2005)
Dedication: *With admiration for Dan J. Marlowe, author of The Name of the Game Is Death: Hardest of the Hardboiled.*
Explanation: Dan J. Marlowe (1917–1986) was a crime fiction author whose work King likes and admires; since *The Colorado Kid* was King's first full-fledged crime novel, dedicating it to a predecessor who had inspired him was only fitting.

Book: *Cell* (Scribner, 2006)
Dedication: *For Richard Matheson and George Romero*
Explanation: When King writes his first novel about an apocalypse turning humans into mindless and murderous monsters, it is hardly surprising that he dedicates it to two artists who have pioneered that notion: George A. Romero (1940–2017), whose *Night of the Living*

Dead inspired the later surge of zombie horror movies, and Richard Matheson (1926–2013), whose 1954 novel *I Am Legend* heralded both the resurgence of vampire stories and, later, the zombie revival.

Book: *Lisey's Story* (Scribner, 2006)
Dedication: *For Tabby*
Explanation: When Stephen King writes a novel about the widow of a successful writer after his death tries to simultaneously move on with her life and remember her repressed insights about her husband, to whom should he dedicate it if not his wife Tabitha? Particularly since his inspiration for the book was his discovery that she while he had been hospitalized had emptied out his writing room, and thought, ”this is how it will look after I die.”

Book: Blaze (as Richard Bachman, Scribner, 2007)
Dedication: *For Tommy and Lori Spruce. And thinking of James T. Farrell*
Explanation: Tommy Spruce is Tabitha King's brother. James T. Farrell (1904–1979) was a writer, known primarily for his three novels about Studs Lonigan (1932–1935), which Stephen King says he read at the age of twelve.

Book: *Duma Key* (Scribner, 1008)
Dedication: *For Barbara Ann and Jimmy*
Explanation: It isn't generally known who Barbara Ann and Jimmy are; presumably friends of Stephen King.

Book: *Just After Sunset* (Scribner, 2008)
Dedication: *For Heidi Pitlor*
Explanation: Heidi Pitlor is a former senior editor and Houghton Mifflin Harcourt and a novelist. She is the series editor for the annual anthology *The Best American Short Stories*, and Stephen King was her co-editor for the 2007 volume of the series.

Book: *Under the Dome* (Scribner, 2009)
Dedication: *In memory of Surendra Dahyabhai Patel. We miss you, my friend.*
Explanation: King had previously dedicated *From a Buick 8* to his friend Surendra Patel. Patel died in 2008, and was important to King.

Book: *Blockade Billy* (Cemetery Dance, 2010)
Dedication: *This is for every guy (and gal) who ever put on the gear.*
Explanation: A novella about a baseball catcher, dedicated to all baseball players, young and old.

Book: *Full Dark, No Stars* (Scribner, 2010)
Dedication: *For Tabby Still.*
Explanation: A collection of stories, "still" dedicated to Tabitha King.

Book: *11/22/63* (Scribner, 2011)
Dedication: *For Zelda. Hey, honey, welcome to the party.*
Explanation: Zelda is Stephen and Tabitha King's youngest son Joe's daughter.

Book: *The Wind Through the Keyhole* (Scribner, 2012)
Dedication: *This is for Robin Furth, and the gang at Marvel Comics.*
Explanation: A thank you to Robin Furth, King's research assistant, who for many years had the task of keeping track of all characters, dates, events, and places in his "Dark Tower" series. She later published two concordances to the series, and was involved in writing the comics inspired by the series. That an unexpected eight "Dark Tower" book would be dedicated to her must be considered only fair.

Book: *Joyland* (Hard Case, 2013)
Dedication: *For Donald Westlake*
Explanation: A crime novel, dedicated to leading crime fiction author Donald Westlake (1933–2008), whom Stephen King admired;

the villain of King's novel *The Dark Half*, George Stark, was named for Westlake's pseudonym Richard Stark, and King asked Westlake's permission to use the name.

Book: *Doctor Sleep* (Scribner, 2013)
Dedication: *When I was playing my primitive brand of rhythm guitar with a group called the Rock Bottom Remainders, Warren Zevon used to gig with us. Warren loved gray t-shirts and movies like Kingdom of the Spiders. He insisted I sing lead on his signature tune, "Werewolves of London," during the encore portion of our shows. I said I was not worthy. He insisted that I was. "Key of G," Warren told me, "and howl like you mean it. Most important of all: play like Keith." I'll never be able to play like Keith Richards, but I always did my best, and with Warren beside me, matching me note for note and laughing his fool head off, I always did my best. Warren this howl is for you, wherever you are. I miss you, buddy.*
Explanation: A self-explanatory dedication. Warren Zevon died from lung cancer in 2012.

Book: *Mr. Mercedes* (Scribner, 2014)
Dedication: *Thinking of James M. Cain. They threw me off the hay truck about noon …*
Explanation: James M. Cain (1892–1977) was a critically hailed and popular novelist, considered one of the progenitors of the hardboiled school of crime fiction. The quote in the dedication is from Cain's most famous novel, *The Postman Always Rings Twice*.

Book: *Revival* (Scribner, 2014)
Dedication: *This is for the people who built my house:*
Mary Shelley
Bram Stoker
H. P. Lovecraft
Clark Ashton Smith
Donald Wandrei
Fritz Leiber

August Derleth
Shirley Jackson
Robert Bloch
Peter Straub
And ARTHUR MACHEN, whose short novel "The Great God Pan" has haunted me all my life.
Explanation: The authors listed are all central to the development and different schools of modern horror literature. Welshman Arthur Machen (1863–1947) is viewed as one of the finest of all horror authors; King has described "The Great God Pan" as "Maybe the best [horror story] in the English language."

Book: *Finders Keepers* (Scribner, 2015)
Dedication: *Thinking of John D. MacDonald*
Explanation: John D. MacDonald (1916–1986) was an immensely popular and critically acclaimed writer of both mainstream and crime novels and stories. He wrote the introduction to Stephen King's first short story collection, *Night Shift.* They remained friends until MacDonald's death. King has called him "the great entertainer of our age", but also said that MacDonald "taught me everything I know."

Book: *End of Watch* (Scdribner, 2016)
Dedication: *For Thomas Harris*
Explanation: Thomas Harris is both a friend and a fellow writer; both Harris and King have sneaked in references to each other's work in some of their books. In *End of Watch*, a character named Fredricka Bimmel is borrowed from Harris' most famous novel, *The Silence of the Lambs.*

Book: *Hearts in Suspension* (University of Maine Press, 2016)
Dedication: *For Burton Hatlen, Edward "Ted" Holmes, and Edward "Sandy" Ives, in memoriam.*
In part a reiteration of the dedication in *The Long Walk*, where Explanation: King thanks Hatlen and Holmes, both once his teachers at the University of Maine. Ives, too, taught at the university.

Book: *Sleeping Beauties* (with Owen King, Scribner, 2017)
Dedication: *In remembrance of Sandra Bland*
Explanation: Sandra Annette Bland was a 28-years old African-American woman who was found hanged in a prison cell in Waller County, Texas, on July 13, 2015, three days after she was arrested for a minor infraction during a traffic stop. Her death was officially called a suicide, which led to protests since many viewed the entire episode as racist abuse.

Book: *The Outsider* (Scribner, 2018)
Dedication: *For Rand and Judy Holston*
Explanation: Rand Holston handles Stephen King's film rights and is a friend.

Book: *Elevation* (Scribner, 2018)
Dedication: *Thinking of Richard Matheson*
Explanation: Richard Matheson has figured in earlier dedications; he was in important horror writer whom King has called "the author who influenced me the most as a writer."

Book: *The Institutet* (Scribner, 2019)
Dedication: *For my grandsons: Ethan, Aidan, and Ryan.*
Explanation: The three boys mentioned are all sons of Joe Hill.

Book: *If It Bleeds* (Scribner, 2020)
Dedication: *Thinking of Russ Dorr, I miss you, Chief.*
Explanation: Russ Dorr was a physician's assistant as well as Stephen King's researcher on all things medical, advisor and close friend for more than thirty years. He died shortly before the book was published.

Book: *Later* (Hard Case, 2021)
Dedication: *For Chris Lotts*
Explanation: Chris Lotts was an assistant to Stephen King's foreign literary agent Ralph Vicinanza; after Vicinanza's sudden death in

2010, Lotts first rand the Vicinanza agency for a short period, then formed his own agency and retained many of Vicinanza's clients, including Stephen King.

Book: *Billy Summers* (Scribner, 2021)
Dedication: *Thinking of Raymond and Sarah Jane Spruce*
Explanation: The Spruces were Tabitha King's parents.

Book: *Gwendy's Final Task* (with Richard Chizmar, Cemetery Dance, 2022)
Dedication: *For Marsha DeFilippo, a friend to a couple of writers*
Explanation: Marsha DeFilippo for nearly 33 years was Stephen King's personal assistant. After retiring, in June, 2020, she has published several novels.

Book: *Fairy Tale* (Scribner, 2022)
Dedication: *Thinking of REH, ERB, and, of course, HPL*
Explanation: The three sets of initials stand for Robert E. Howard (1906–1936), creator of Conan and writer of what is known as "sword and sorcery" fantasy; Edgar Rice Burroughs (1875–1950), creator of Tarzan and many other adventure story heroes; H. P. Lovecraft (1890–1937), an influential cult author of horror fantasy stories. *Fairy Tale* can be said to incorporate elements from all three.

Book: *Holly* (Scribner, 2023)
Dedication: *This is for Chuck Verrill. Editor, agent, and most of all, friend. 1951–2022. Thanks, Chuck.*
Explanation: Stephen King's literary agent and friend; he died January 9, 2022.

Book: *You Like It Darker* (Scribner, 2024)
Dedication: *For the twins, Thomas and Edward*
Explanation: Thomas and Edward are twins to Joe Hill in his second marriage. This also makes them Stephen King's fifth and sixth grandchild.

Book: *Never Flinch* (Scribner, 2025)
Dedication: *For Robin Furth, with love and thanks for all your hard work.*
Explanation: Robin Furth began working as a researcher for King when he began writing volumes five, six, and seven of The Dark Tower series. She later helped him also with research for other books and with other tasks.

www.ingramcontent.com/pod-product-compliance
Ingram Content Group UK Ltd.
Pitfield, Milton Keynes, MK11 3LW, UK
UKHW021909190726
13853UKWH00002B/592